New Mountain Man

New Mountain Man

Stories Of Living Alone In An Old Log Cabin
In The Southern Appalachians

Beaumont R. Hagebak

Deeds Publishing | Athens

Published by Deeds Publishing in Athens, GA
www.deedspublishing.com

Printed in The United States of America

Cover design by Mark Babcock.

ISBN 978-1-947309-59-3

Books are available in quantity for promotional or premium use. For information, email info@deedspublishing.com.

First Edition, 2020

10 9 8 7 6 5 4 3 2 1

This book of stories is dedicated to my three sons: Haakon, Christen, and Beaumont William, and to the people they love and cherish. Raised in the same household, my sons have lived very different lives. One is a retired insurance company executive who, like his father, has recently moved back to Georgia and who has dealt with and overcome many obstacles to success. Another is a fine artist and a wonderful teacher, who does both in his own studio in a mid-sized Georgia town and is building an international reputation for the quality of his work. The last served in the U.S. Coast Guard and then began a career with a metropolitan police force where he advanced from a motorcycle officer to become Captain of the force. He is now retired, writing books of his own. They know me well, those boys and their families. They know that I love them.

—**Beaumont R. Hagebak,** Father

Contents

Foreword

The echoes of bellowing laughter fill our hearts and minds like a warm autumn breeze blowing passionately from a little bend of the world known as Corner Oak Court. Laughter was the most commonplace display of emotion for those who knew the author of the work on the following pages. The act of laughter has been proven time and time again to be an antidote for depression, fear, anger, and most other ailments of modern life.

As a psychologist, humorist, and author, Beaumont "Ace" Hagebak knew this fact well in advance of the recent studies and wielded humor like a Viking wields an axe, hacking away at the negativity of the world and bringing joy to anyone and everyone in his modest audience.

Not surprisingly, that audience broadened with each person he met. No matter how brief the contact, the spectators of his spoken words were immediately disarmed by the author's humor, caring, and genuine grace. Like most psychologists, he was a master of the spoken word, drawing his subjects to find themselves deep within his perspectives and stories. As a college professor, he enjoyed his time in the lectern. Students and faculty alike would pay close attention to his lectures for their sage nuggets of information revealed in captivating humor.

When he worked for the Public Health Service, his ability to lead meetings were legendary, mixing well timed jokes with the critical matters of the day. The brief audiences, like the grocery store clerks, pharmacists, and shop owners learned of him quickly. His reputation preceded him wherever he went. To family and friends, his conversations were naturally more intimate. He was frank with his emotions and quick to empathy, he was a joy with which to speak.

As you'll discover in the pages that follow, the spoken word was not his sole gift. If you were fortunate enough to see his paintings and drawings, you already know he was talented with watercolors, ink, and oils, but his ability to paint with the written word is now the stuff of legend. In the late 1970s, he wrote the book, *Getting Local Agencies to Cooperate*. It was a small instructional piece, with his illustration of a pudgy Viking serving as a sort of mascot, introducing each chapter. It was a serious professional work, used for a few years by many students and bureaucrats alike to help improve public sector work. That work was his first beyond college assignments.

From the time of completing his first book, he began to write incessantly, mostly stories of his life and observations. Not surprisingly, his writing style was conversational and almost without exception, humorous. He wrote frequently, sending them on to we lucky few on his mailing list.

It was this "daily mail" that now rests in your hands. He wrote 130 page-long tales and observations from his first year in his log cabin in North Georgia. He lived there for nearly two years, alone, but not lonely, in the woods. His neighbors adopted him as the philosopher on the corner, one having written a song of him, "The Wizard of Corner Oak Court". Friends, family, and neighbors would stop by frequently to share a glass of wine, a story, and a laugh.

As you leaf the pages that follow, if you're able to enjoy a cheap glass of red wine and slice of cheese, the old bear who lived in the woods and wrote these words for you would be honored. If you find yourself chuckling, do not laugh quietly, let your laughs billow through the trees as the words move from the page into your heart and mind. As was the author's habit to honor his Nordic heritage with a simple toast, flip the page, lift your glass high in the air and yell, "SKOL!"

—**Haakon Hagebak,** Son of the author

Dear Ace,

I cannot begin to tell you how much I enjoyed reading about your first year in a log cabin in the woods, in the North Georgia mountains, here on Corner Oak Court. Although I found it enlightening to learn about your life and the circumstances the led you to our street, it is your impact on this neighborhood that fascinates me most. It took a great deal of courage to face this first year living alone and a determined commitment to stick to the task of facing and documenting the emotional truth of your new reality. And, for as much as I as a reader learned about you, it must pale in comparison with everything you have learned about yourself.

Hopefully you see what I see. That you are a product of eighty-one years of life's experiences...making you the closest thing I know of to an expert on the world around us. Your words paint masterpieces that I can see and touch and relate. You find fascinating subjects to paint in the most unusual places, and need not look much farther than your own yard to take incredible journeys into the inner thoughts of your imagination. I was happy to be a part of those journeys.

Most importantly, as I read more and more, a picture of you in your log cabin became more and more clear. Soon I began to think of you as both literally and figuratively, the CORNER of Corner Oak Court. You have brought your eighty-one years of experience and taken up sentry duty to the entrance of our street. We see you, or at the very least, your house every day. Each person on our street has learned something from you and perhaps has added a little something to your experiences. Consequently, you have become a fixture on our street and we are all better people for knowing you.

It is an awesome responsibility to be the CORNER of Corner Oak Ct., but the "Old Bear in his Log Lair" is more than suited to that task.

Thanks for sharing,

Mark Taylor

2018

So ... What The Heck Is This?

This is a book written in the first person singular by a male person in his early eighties, who is single and living in an old log cabin in an oak forest in the foothills of the North Georgia mountains. The fact that the author is single after almost forty years of marriage is the key to understanding his relocation from northern California to northern Georgia, his purchase of an old log home, and a new way of living. It's his story and he's sticking to it!

My Story: I grew up in Minnesota and lived for a time way up by Lake Superior, before I realized that I could be warmer. So, we moved to Georgia. I lived with my wives (two, but sequentially) and my sons (three, also sequentially) in Georgia for about forty years before moving to California to be near my second wife's little two-year-old granddaughter. For a long, long time my wife had lived near my sons and my five granddaughters (never did have any grandsons, but all the granddaughters were delights to the eye and the spirit). Long enough to have four great-grandsons and one little great-granddaughter. So, making the move seemed fair.

We spent six years in California, having a wonderful time with good friends and neighbors and lots of stuff to see and do. And then, one night, my wife asked for a divorce. Well, she didn't really ask, she told me. I tried to talk her out of it for a solid month. Even played the sympathy card: "I'm more than eighty years old. I'll die soon. Can't you wait awhile?" Nothing worked. Time to make some lemonade out of this lemon I'd been handed.

We parted amicably enough, having divided up our possessions, our finances, and probably our friends as well. These things can be hard on friends. I started packing and losing weight. Moving cardboard boxes full of amazing wonders was the most exercise I'd had in years. A good buddy and I drove to Georgia, where my sons and an old log cabin I had planned to rent were waiting for me. Paid the first month's rent. The moving van arrived, my half of our life together was hauled into the cabin, and I was exhausted!! (Remember, I'm no spring chicken!) And I said to myself, "Self, you are *not* ever going to do this again!!" And so I bought the place!!

These are my stories about a full year from that moment on. Hope you'll enjoy them. You'll find pathos, deep philosophical issues, and humor. Lots of humor. Enjoy. It's really all true.

New Mountain Man

1. The Mountains That Are Home

Let's talk of a small Georgia town about an hour or so north of Atlanta which is home to beautiful Lake Arrowhead, nestled in the foothills and mountains of the southern Appalachian chain; of the Lake Arrowhead community of 8,000 acres and just over 1,000 homes, only three of them built of logs long before the community was incorporated; of the history of the area and the "lost town" that now lies under the lake; and let's talk, too, of ghosts.

Small Towns

You know the old joke: "That town was so small that they put the city limits signs on the same pole." Waleska, Georgia, is just a bit larger than that. It's the town closest to my log cabin in the woods. I choose to live in or near small towns. Something about the rural lifestyle appeals to me. Maybe it's the friendliness, the willingness to share, the unlocked doors, the quiet evenings, the wildlife to be seen and enjoyed.

I was once told by a college student from New York City that I was not doing right by my three sons because the town we lived in was small.

Exposure to what he called "the real world" was the only way to raise children. Somehow, we all did just fine. Rich, full lives, filled with friends of every description. Life has not always been easy for each of us, but life is never always easy for anyone, whether it's lived in a small town or a huge city.

Cities have their charms, sure. Activities of all kinds attract us, unbelievable options are available day and night, services of all kinds are right nearby when we need or want them. There's the freedom that anonymity can bring. But for some of us, rural communities offer so much more. Big lifetime words, like peace and contentment. Nature's doorstep is our doorstep, too. And there are always people who won't look the other way when a neighbor needs help. You're known.

Today our work often defines our locations and our lifestyles. Young people, in particular, leave their rural homes for employment in large cities. Small towns suffer as farms grow larger and farm people who once patronized local shops are forced to move away. But the special joys of small-town living don't disappear. And our small towns wait for those who love them to return.

Lake Arrowhead, Georgia? Never Heard Of It!

I'd flown from California to Atlanta in mid-December to watch my son, Haakon, retire from the Cobb County, Georgia, police department as a Captain. Impressive! And given the times we live in, timely, too! When things settled down a bit he asked me, "Well, dad, what are you going to do now?" I would soon be a divorcee, so it was a natural enough question. "Thought I'd move back to Georgia to be closer to my own family, maybe up in the Big Canoe area or something." I had heard rumors that my two Georgia daughters-in-law were looking into assisted living facilities for me, so I needed to get proactive fast! "You don't want to do that, dad", the ex-police Captain said. "Big Canoe's too far away. You want to consider Lake Arrowhead." "What's at Lake Arrowhead?" I asked. "Come on. We'll drive up and take a look."

Forty minutes later, we were there in the North Georgia mountains! "Wow. 8,000 acres of lush woodland, much of it old oak forest! We drove by the lake first. Clear and clean, mountain stream fed, 540 acres of sparkling blue water! No speedboats allowed. The marina is home to small sailboats, canoes, and lots of pontoon boats, both privately owned and rentals. Fishing is great, they say. Higher up we passed the eighteen-hole Highlands Golf Course, and a 10,000 square foot clubhouse with both indoor and outdoor dining. The "Great Festival Park" boasts a Junior Olympic pool, basketball courts, volleyball, batting cages, a playground for the little kids, and a pavilion. The Lake Arrowhead community has over eight miles of hiking trails, some right on the lakeshore. There's a new firehouse manned by local volunteers, and a community church. It's a gated community with guards on the gates 'round the clock. No crime to speak of. It's all within striking distance of the brand-new Northside Cherokee Hospital, which opened its doors in early May 2017. A couple of miles down the road is the historic little town of Waleska, with Reinhardt University and the Falany Performing Arts Center. Mountain air, and a climate roughly five or ten degrees cooler than Atlanta on any given day. About 900 homes, some of them rentals, but only three old log cabins, including mine. I bought one of those three and a nice piece of the wilderness surrounding it for far less than the asking price for most homes in the community. Great people live here and introduce me to their friends as "the guy who lives in the old log cabin up on the corner of Corner Oak Court." And so I do.

I do believe that with the help of my families here in Georgia, and the advice of my son Haakon (folks call him "Hawk" because there are precious few Norwegians in Georgia and he was having to explain the double "a" every time he'd meet somebody new), and a great real estate agent, I have landed on a spot on the face of this old Earth that is just about perfect for this old country boy.

Maybe Just A Wee Bit Of History?

Back in 1856, a gentleman named John B. Puckett (1806-1883) bought a large piece of land, 760 acres, in Cherokee County, Georgia, to develop a plantation. There he built a "mansion" for his family, complete with glass windows, white gravel walkways, and some beautiful pure white ducks. His home was set in a fertile valley because the rich land there was just right for growing cotton and corn. A cold mountain spring brought pure, clear water to the family. A massive log barn was also built to hold farm animals and the produce that grew so well in the valley, mainly corn. Mr. Puckett put some of that corn to use at a corn "likker" still he made in a cave on his property.

By 1878, county tax records show that his land was valued at $3,000 and the family household furnishings (including a piano), tools, pictures, books, and livestock were valued at $345, making the Puckett family the wealthiest in the district. The family grew and prospered, and John's wife, Jane, gave birth to at least three children on the place. One of them, a young girl named Victoria, had her own horse. When a group of Yankee soldiers came through the area and confiscated her horse, it is said that she gave chase and her horse was returned to her!

Over time, a small town, "Lost Town" sprang up in the area now covered by Lake Arrowhead. There were at least twenty-one homes in the fertile mountain valley. But later, the Puckett mansion burned to the ground and a much smaller home was built on the land it once occupied. Eventually, a large paper company bought all the property and removed all the buildings, leaving just one chimney. Today, that chimney is standing somewhere beneath man-made Lake Arrowhead. All that remains of the town now are the records of its existence, the family wills, and tax records, kept in the Cherokee County Courthouse.

Ghosts!!?

I do not believe in ghosts. Let's get that straight right at the beginning. But "Putih", my big black cat does! For sure! And because she does, it can get a little weird around here.

Today is a good example. Old "Putih" has climbed into my lap at least five times, and it's only mid-afternoon. She's got these huge eyes, and from my lap she looks behind me, wide-eyed, into the dining area, the upstairs, and the hallway to the guest bedrooms. When I say "wide-eyed", I mean looking like she's seen a ghost! Even though I am an unbeliever, I really feel the hair on the back of my neck rise (which is odd in itself, since I had a haircut just yesterday and there are no hairs on the back of my neck!), and more often than not I actually turn around to look, too!

On the outside wall of my cabin in the woods there is a plaque, brass I think, placed there by some owner who came before me. The plaque reads: "On this spot in 1897, nothing happened." I'm willing to buy into that, but what about 1887, or 1877, or more likely 1755 or 1864?? What about that? Oh, there's plenty of reason to think there might be ghosts around my old cabin, IF (I capitalized "IF" on purpose) you believe in ghosts like my cat does.

For example, in 1879, ancient Native American petroglyphs were discovered in Waleska, just three miles down the road. Could those earliest Americans have had homes right here on my land? In 1755, the Creek and Cherokee nations battled one another in Ball Ground, a few miles from here. The Cherokee won. (Parenthetically—whatever that means—I once knew a Creek Indian Princess, but that was long ago and far away.) The gold rush got here in 1819 out at Sixes Mill, now Sixes Road, where my doctors work. The town I drive twelve miles to for shopping, Canton, was burned by Sherman in October of 1864, despite the fact that this county was pro-Union! The Civil War battle of Resaca, near here, was fought on May 14, 1864, and Cartersville, not far from here, fell to Sherman's forces on May 23 of that year. And the Battle of New Hope Church, twenty-five miles northwest of Atlanta, was won by Sherman, too. Hey! 101 Corner Oak Court is about twenty-five miles northwest of Atlanta!! (Maybe a bit more, but who's counting?)

So, from ancient rock sculptors to gold prospectors to Civil War soldiers, any number of people could have walked through my yard, or even through what is now my home. There may have been tents pitched here. People may have lived and died in what I now call my front yard. And I supposed it's just possible that my cat knows more about such things than I do. Sometimes it's a blessing NOT to know stuff. This may be one of those times.

I think of myself as being a "romantic" of sorts, more of a poet and dreamer than I am a modern man invested in technology. Oh, I don't believe in ghosts, of course. I'm at least THAT modern. But when "Putih" crawls up into my lap, and peers out behind me to check out this old cabin, I will probably always look and will hopefully always see nothing. I really want to see nothing!! I'm just not ready to change my nonbelief in ghosts, in spite of my big old black cat and in spite of this old cabin in the woods!

2. This Wonderful Old Log Cabin

A description of the cabin itself; learning what works and what doesn't work; getting to know the thermostat, the toilets, the huge old gas fireplace, the unique "Grandmother" and "Grandfather" guest bedrooms; and the name given to the cabin by family. The "bam, whang, groan" sounds that you may hear aren't really ghoulies and ghosties but are caused by temperature changes. You'll still jump.

Meeting My Log Cabin For The Very First Time

When most folks move from one place to another, something gets left behind. Happens all the time. There's always a forgotten picture or a plaque, or a teacup, or maybe even a lawn trimmer. There's always something. And some things are left behind on purpose!

When I walked into my old log cabin for the very first time there were still some pictures on the walls and some "sayings" here and there, some even done in brass. I had plenty of pictures. My dad was an artist who worked in oils, and several of his paintings now grace my new home. I'm an artist of sorts, too. I have a self-portrait in my underwear above the toilet in my bedroom "suite", in the style of Leonardo da Vinci, which only select people are given an opportunity to see. Most of the pictures that were left here have been taken down and stored in the shed. But there were some wonderful philosophical statements that I kept right where I found them.

Above the guest toilet, for example, is a one-word plaque that shouts "SIMPLIFY", all in caps. I am not at all sure how one simplifies time on the toilet, and probably don't want to know. In a hallway, there is an ornate plaque that states, top to bottom, "Relax, Reflect, Review". Good advice, but I would have put "Relax" after "Reflect" and "Review" because, at my advanced age, if you reflect on the life you've led and review the things you did, you NEED to "Relax"!! But just inside the main door to the cabin, on the way up the stairs to my art studio, photo library, and bedroom, there was left behind a very ornate brass plaque that grabs my attention every time I pass by it. It says, *"Life isn't about waiting for the storm to pass. Life is about learning to dance in the rain."* Great Truth, on a log wall.

Every woman I have ever had the opportunity to dance with, rain or shine, including my high school girlfriend, my first wife, my second wife, and a few delightful ladies in between, will tell you that I cannot dance! My stoic Norwegian heritage runs deep—all the way down to my feet! But when I saw that plaque, well before the moving van arrived, I knew I'd found the right place for me. I need to learn to dance, and I am practicing in the rain. Life is about that. So says the plaque, and so say I.

The Thermostat

Thermostats are brilliant creatures. They assess the degree of warmth or coolness in a room (or in the case of this North Georgia mountain cabin of mine, in the whole blame house!) and then, knowing what temperature you want in the place, they tell the air conditioner or the heating unit to get with the program.

The thermostat in this old log cabin was dealing with some severe handicapping conditions when I moved in. First, it was hanging loose on the wall of the dining area, sort of looking down at the floor. Second, it was sharing that wall with a gas burning auxiliary space heater that had a working pilot light—a gas flame on all the time. That pilot light was about three feet below the thermostat, which looked down at it. The pilot light warmed the air upward well beyond the thermostat. So...if the thermostat was set to turn on the air conditioning at 72 degrees Fahrenheit, it felt to the thermostat that the temperature in the cabin was about 83 degrees! I had to set the thermostat at 86 degrees in order to fool it into ordering the air conditioner to shut down!

Daytime and evening temperatures vary a good bit in these mountains, so confusion reigned!! I needed help. Help arrived in the form of a young fella, couldn't have been more than fifteen years old (well, to these eighty-year-old eyes everyone's a "kid"), by the name of Ryan. "Most folks want to call me Bryan, with a 'B', but it's Ryan with an 'R'!" He worked outside to assure that my heating and air conditioning systems were in good shape. "I've never seen a system that old working that well," reported Ryan. (Wish my doctors would say the same about me!) And then Ryan spent about an hour, and I spent $65.00, rewiring and relocating the thermostat to a wall in the hallway.

My thermostat is working just fine now, thank you. It is once again a brilliant creature, and I am quite comfortable day and night.

The New Toilets

When you visit a kindergarten classroom (if you never have, you should give it a try 'cause it's a barrel of fun!) you expect to find little tiny toilets.

But not in a log cabin where a fully grown old man lives. Toilets there should be built for grown-ups. There should be a law. (Lots of "shoulds" in that short paragraph. Sorry. But right is right and wrong is wrong!!)

And so I was shocked to find that someone had installed kindergarten-level toilets in both of my grown-up bathrooms. I suppose I should have been thankful that they were indoors at least. Some cabins up here in the North Georgia mountains have a trail and a separate little house with lots of magazines, and those magazines are not necessarily for reading. No running water, either. Once upon a time my very first mother-in-law walked the trail from a little northern Minnesota vacation cabin we'd rented to the little house out back (probably why they call them "out-houses") at night. She opened the door, and there was a *bear* using the facility!! Not sure just which of them was most frightened, but I'm guessing it was the bear.

But I digress. Every time I had to use the toilets (either one) in my cabin, my arthritic knees rebelled against my efforts to stand back up! I was always afraid that some friend, not having seen me for several days and concerned that something bad had happened to me, would come in search of me, open the bathroom door (either one) and there I would be, pants down around my ankles, struggling to stand. I prayed that it would be a male friend, although I am pleased and proud to say that I do have some female friends up here in the North Georgia forest.

So I hired a plumber, told him I wanted the tallest toilets in the nation, and sent him out to find them. He found them, all right! Those two new toilets cost more than my complete dining room set, with six chairs and a leaf to extend the table! I let the plumber take the old toilets with him at no extra charge.

And now I can stand up from either toilet without using my cane. No problem!

My Old Fireplace: It's A "Gas"

This old log cabin boasts a ten-foot wide stone fireplace. The stonework could have been better, but it's still quite a fireplace. It uses gas logs. The smell isn't the same as burning oak gives off, and there's no "snap, crackle, pop" that makes a wood fire so much fun to watch, but there aren't any ashes to haul off either.

I always worry about gas, though, ever since I saw a house blow up in Minnesota and blast out windows in stores downtown a quarter of a mile away! But it got pretty cool one evening in March, so I turned the gas logs on. Within minutes the living room was warm and toasty. I turned away to check something on my computer, and when I turned back *the fire had gone out*!! OH, GEE WHIZ!!! I dashed over to the fireplace and fiddled around with the switch until I was convinced that the gas was shut off.

A few hours later, my youngest son showed up to check on his dad. "Dad, I think I smell gas." He fiddled around with a switch at the other end of the gas line, and got that end dealt with to his satisfaction. Major crisis averted. I vowed never again would I turn that fireplace on, *never*!

A month or so later, a strange car came up the driveway. A nice-looking couple got out and walked up to my door. Saw them coming and went to greet them, whoever they were. It turned out that the guy was a former owner of the cabin and sold it five years earlier to the lady I bought it from. He'd built the patio and the fire pit outside. Said he had been with the F.B.I. "What the heck was an F.B.I man doing living in this cabin in the North Georgia woods?" I asked myself. The only answer that I could come up with was that he was probably in some witness protection program. I treated him with new respect after I sort of figured that out.

He and his wife wandered through my home, at my invitation. Eventually we came to the huge old fireplace. He said, looking at the gas logs,

"You know, I put a thermostat in that fireplace when I lived here, and when the place got warm enough, the thermostat shut the gas off."

OH, FOR PETE'S SAKE! The fireplace was MEANT to go out after twenty minutes or so! I never would have figured that out. Never! And now I have to get the gas company guy out here to pull that thermostat so my guests and I can enjoy a nice, warming fire for more than a few minutes at a time. If it isn't one thing, it's another. Life in a cabin in the north woods is always a special experience!

The Guest Bedrooms

During my first week of living here, the cabin walls were covered with paintings done by me, my dad, and even some other people, and I still had a stack of "stuff" three feet high. In that stack was a large oval photo of my great-grandfather, Ole, wearing his bear skin hat and his buffalo robe, handsome and dignified (getting your picture taken in the 1800's was clearly a serious business!). He was a Hagebak. There was also a large photo in a matching oval frame of my grandmother, Anne, who died before I was born. She was a Mork. Grandpa Mork went to church the first Sunday after arriving in Minnesota from Norway, saw her wearing a blue dress, and without even meeting her, told the family he was temporarily staying with, that he had met the girl he was going to marry. And he did. He insisted that all of their daughters had to wear blue dresses, too!

There was a painting of a great ape, thinking. There was large watercolor of a girl in Norway, in full Norwegian dress; a group of Ford cars painted by a college friend; my grandfather Mork's cane with a likeness of his head carved on top, and my grandfather Hagebak's pipe. I remember him smoking it, but never filling it. Hold a modern pipe up next to it and you'll see that grandpa's pipe was HUGE! There were "artifacts" of all kinds—grandpa Mork's citizenship certificate renouncing his allegiance to the King of Norway, a beautiful little teacup from England, a large German beer mug from my Army days, a Haitian voodoo box with tiny dolls in it, a rhino tooth from my dad's dental office that he used to teach his patients about enamel and tooth decay, and much more. When you're the oldest living Hagebak, as I am, you tend to become the caretaker for lots of "stuff".

And then it dawned on me: make one of the guest bedrooms into a "Grandfathers Room", and the other matching guest bedroom into a "Grandmothers Room". I sorted paintings and artifacts into two piles, one quite masculine, the other quite feminine. I had a bit of trouble deciding what to do with the voodoo box but remembered that it had been given to me by a beautiful and gifted female physician who once worked for me in the U.S. Public Health Service. It went into the "Grandmothers Room".

I ordered matching shelves to hold some of the artifacts, and matching nightstands to hold books I had written about my mother and her family, and about my father and his family. I put up photos of my mother, and other mothers in the family, and even asked for and got a photo of my first wife, the mother of my three sons, and the grandmother of their daughters. I put up photos of grandfathers, including one of myself in my Army uniform taken ages before I ever had a thought in my head about becoming a grandfather. Somehow, each of the guest bedrooms came together well. Visiting family and friends enjoy checking out each of the rooms and its contents.

So now, if you should visit this old log cabin in the North Georgia Mountains, and plan to stay the night, you will have a choice to make. The Grandfathers Room? The Grandmothers Room? They are mirror images of one another—same bed, same nightstand, same chair, same closet, same window on the world—but different artwork on the walls, different photos, different books, and different bits and pieces of the lives led by our family. I hope that both bedrooms are worthy of your exploration. There are items of interest for both children and adults, just like everywhere else in this, my forest home.

Signs (No Portents, Though)

Years ago, we had a mountain home that we called "Fjellhavn", Norwegian for "Mountain Harbor". It was our harbor, our weekend get-away, a place where friends could come to relax. We had a sign made for the driveway entry that identified the place for all comers. The name was a good one, a name with real meaning, and very Norwegian.

Early in my new life in this old log cabin I now call home, the question of an appropriate name came up. Relatives and friends understood that this refuge couldn't be called "Fjellhavn". That name was already used and had a special link to place and time. The name of this home had to be different, but meaningful, and still very Norwegian, of course.

I suppose I'd gotten a bit shaggy looking since moving to North Georgia from California. No real need for a fancy haircut up here in the mountains. My stride was slow and ponderous, not at all like the way I walked as a younger man. Watching me work around the place, a son said, "Y'know, dad, you look a lot like a bear, an old bear. Maybe we could call this home of yours 'the old bear's den'." There were grins all around, and the name stuck.

In Norwegian, "the old bear's lair" translates into "DEN GAMLE BJØRNEN LEIR". The line (/) through the O in BJORNEN, gives it the authentic Norske touch. When the huge old black bear came walking through the yard last week, I again thought of the sign for the entry to the driveway. I'm having one made.

There are still a few technical details to be worked out. I visualize a sort of rustic sign, made of wood, with the name carved into it using a router. But there are other options. I'm going to look around the yard to see if one of the fallen tree branches might be suitable. There's a dark stained board I found in the laundry room that would certainly work out fine. No rush. I plan to be here a while. I am, after all, the "old bear".

And Things That Go "Bump" In The Night...

Medieval English peasants had a little prayer they would say before going to bed after a hard day's work: "From ghoulies, and ghosties, and long-leggity beasties, and things that go 'bump' in the night, Good Lord, deliver us!"

This old cabin talks! It burps, and belches, and sets off firecrackers! It grunts, and groans, and generally sounds a lot like me, actually. People who know about old log cabins tell me that those sounds are created by the expansion and contraction of the logs as the heat of the day meets the cool of the night. Sounds sensible. But maybe that's just a way of trying to explain away the supernatural. This old cabin of mine is *alive*. Trust me on that. It's *alive*!

I plunk myself down in my recliner after a hard day of cooking, cleaning, painting, writing, and creature feeding, and within minutes there is a "BANG!" at the side door not far from my chair. Sometimes there are two: "BANG, BANG!!" The first week I was here I would leap up half a foot in the air (not a bad trick for a guy who has to use a cane to get around, even in the house). It took me more than a week to realize that those noises were just my old cabin talking to me. After a couple of months living in my cabin, I even stopped going to bed with the lights on. I can now sleep right through "BANG, WHAM, GROAN". Some nights I only have to wake up twice, and that's to go to the bathroom, which for a fellow my age is a real victory.

Last night, though, there was a new sound: "THUMP"! It was at the double doors that lead from my upstairs bedroom to a little balcony.

And since I sleep in the upstairs bedroom, a 'THUMP" just outside those double doors is particularly worrisome. 'THUMP" again! "OK", I told myself, "if it happens again, just one more time, I'm getting out of this bed and over to those double doors with my trusty flashlight." "THUMP!" Damn! Grabbed the flashlight, pulled back the curtains on those double doors, and…NOTHING WAS THERE!! (Good Lord, deliver us!) I closed the curtains, checked to make sure those double doors were locked, and crept back to bed. Not another sound the rest of the night.

Out on the balcony there is a curved steel rod with a hook at the end, and a steel bird feeder attached to the hook. The whole contraption is on a swivel, so I can twist it on to the balcony to add birdseed and twist it back out so the feeder is hanging over open air. Makes for a much cleaner balcony. And now I realized that the "THUMP" was nothing more than a bird landing on the feeder for a midnight snack. But "THUMP"? What the heck was it, an eagle?? No sparrow, for sure. And so, I am still a bit anxious. But the bird seed is gone. Don't think I'll fill it again.

It's Been Quite A Week, Actually!

You'd think, I guess, that an old man living in a log cabin in the North Georgia mountains would be leading a very quiet life. But really, it's been a fun week in lots of very different ways.

First of all, I got my sign for down by the road. Right now there's a wooden post in a wooden pot that may have held flowers at some time in its life, but no more. Just a few scraggly weeds. The post has store-bought numbers on it: 101. That's my address. My new sign is carved into an old board I found in the cabin, and it says: 101 — DEN GAMLE BJORN-ENS LEIR. The kids named the place "The Old Bear's Lair" (I'm the "old bear" I guess) and I had the sign made in Norwegian. The cabin we used to have up in these mountains was named "Fjellhavn", which translates into "Mountain Harbor", and we all loved that name, but I have a feeling we'll grow into this one, too.

Then the dryer went out on Monday, and Sears couldn't come to fix it until "Monday week", which is Southern for the following Monday, a week from the dryer failure. Still under warranty, so I kind of had to use Sears Home Repair folks. Happily, I did find that I had enough underwear around here to last the week and several days more. Men's underwear. No crisis. Just exciting.

Then, really, really good friends from California showed up at my door. They were expected, and I had friends from Corner Oak Court over for a little afternoon party. Everyone enjoyed meeting everyone else, no politics were talked about so there were no fist fights or hair pulling, and several of the ladies (particularly) were impressed at how I'd arranged things. A couple even said that I should have been an interior decorator. But I was, you know. As a psychologist, I just rearranged people's minds. It's a bit late, at age 81, to change careers now. My dad, the finest dentist in southern Minnesota, wanted me to become a dentist, but I couldn't see myself with my hands in other people's mouths. Actually, my work as a psychologist was probably messier!

Well, by Wednesday or Thursday, I'd gotten the place pretty much back to normal, but I have never been more "pooped" (my mother's expression for "exhaustion"). So I sat down in my recliner and began a book I've wanted to re-read. I do tend to forget what I've read, which keeps my book budget down to a manageable level. Fell asleep in the recliner, though, and woke up suddenly when this cat that owns me leaped up into my ample lap!! I didn't think that would happen until 2021 A.D. or so, but there she was, purring away, demanding to be petted. I guess that's why they call them "pets"? So now we are best pals, this big old cat and me. Cool!

The grocery store had fresh "never frozen" cod yesterday. My people over in Norway love cod, so I love it also. The big flakes are really tasty. I bought a pound, the last they had at the store, and the fish monger (do they still call them that?) tossed in a little piece, free. I had a pound and a quarter. Cooked it all up in butter with special seasonings, had some wild rice and English peas, and ate about half a pound. Comfort food!! Tonight, I'll have a bit more, and the rest has been frozen to await your visit, my friends. ☺

So quite a week, actually. There was more, but I am out of paper and I have to go and eat some cod. Didn't sleep all that well last night, so my recliner may get a bit of use in the early evening unless the cat that owns me has other ideas. Y'all take care now, hear?

A Housewarming Gift

I had an old coffee pot that was a perfectly good coffee pot. Well, that may be an exaggeration. It was pretty tired and didn't do well in the cross-country moving van that took it and a couple of thousand pounds of my other stuff from California to Georgia. A lot of things that begin with "c" had trouble. My *computer*, for example, lost its memory for "Sent" messages. The *cookbooks* were lost in a box for weeks. One of my antique *car* models lost its door handles. The antique *clock* won't chime the hours anymore, but then, it never did. But that old coffee pot still made my kind of coffee—weak, humble, see-right-through-it coffee. People who frequent "Starbucks" would look down their noses at my coffee. My son, Haakon, frequents "Starbucks". He was less than impressed with my old coffee pot and the colored water it made each morning.

So, one day Haakon showed up at the cabin with a fancy wrapped box. "It's your housewarming present from us", he told me. He was so excited that HE opened the box!! Inside was a new-fangled Keurig coffee maker, a one-cup-at-a-time model. You fill your coffee cup with water, pour the water in, insert a small plastic container with coffee makin's in it, push a lever which punctures the plastic container and starts heating the water, and in just seconds you have a steaming hot cup of coffee, fresh brewed. That is, if you remembered to put your coffee cup under the little spigot. Forget to do that and you don't have coffee, you have a royal mess! "Well", he said, "I brought the weakest coffee I could find. See, it says 'Tepid'." (Or something like that. I forget). Says my son, "Go ahead! Try it!" So I tried it. "AAAARGH", I said politely. The coffee reminded me of the coffee my Norwegian father used to drink. If the spoon didn't stand straight up in the stuff, it wasn't strong enough for him. Haakon smiled, and took my old coffee pot home with him. I was left alone with this Keurig thing!

I had been given a dozen little plastic containers of coffee and used every one of them by pouring out half of the just filled cup and replacing that with tap water. If there was anything bad in the tap water, the remaining coffee in the cup would kill it. And then, just as I was about to run out of those little plastic containers, I went grocery shopping (bachelor stuff: frozen dinners, brats, strawberries, wine, beer, crackers, cheese, salted redskin peanuts) and there on a shelf were hundreds of those little plastic containers! All different brands! And one brand had some little plastic containers that said "SMOOTH" in capital letters just like that! "Light roast coffee" it said. I bought a dozen. The next morning, I made a full cup with my Keurig machine. It was good!! I make myself a cup every morning now. Family crisis averted!! If you like "sissy coffee" like I do, get some "SMOOTH" stuff. It's good, and good for ya!!

3. The Joy Of Family And Finding New Friends

I have somehow landed among the finest neighbors anyone could have. The first several stories will tell you about these amazing people. Then you'll learn a bit about my family, my three sons in particular, and their lives in Georgia near me. We are Norwegian-Americans, and so you will learn of a Norwegian historian who is writing a book about the larger extended Hagebak family. You'll be amused as I prepare to revisit my "roots" in Minnesota, and as I plan my first party in the cabin for friends and relatives. You'll learn of the death of a long-time friend, and of his unusual funeral service. Finally, you will find me alone but happy on New Year's Eve to welcome 2018.

Friends

"Make new friends, but keep the old, one is silver and the other gold". So says the old song taught to me by my mother, and so say I. I haven't kept up with my Army buddies, although I wonder about them from time to time. I don't correspond with my college friends, except for my dorm roommate, Paul and his wife, Dixie, and my mentor and friend Cal, and his wife, Jeanette. I stay in touch with many friends out in California, Europe, and elsewhere, and hope that continues forever. Friends from my high school days will always be with me. A large "Fiftieth Reunion" photo in a frame of my class of 1954 back in southern Minnesota sits on my two-drawer lateral file next to the computer, where I can look at their wonderful faces any time I wish. But it's the newfound friends here in the North Georgia mountains that I want to concentrate on just now. By some stroke of extremely good fortune, I happen to have settled in the first home on Corner Oak Court, the friendliest street in all of Lake Arrowhead.

It began with my real estate agent, Jamie, who went to extremes to make sure I got to see the inside of this home before I moved in. He made a fine video of the place, just for me. He welcomed me when the moving van and I arrived, and he and his partner, Javier, came by to help me hang pictures and rearrange furniture the next day. A glass of white wine, a beer, nothing asked, and nothing wanted except my friendship. I began to believe I'd chosen the right spot in the world. A couple of days later, there was a knock on my door. Margaret, a Scottish lady with a brogue that makes her unique, was at the door with a pot of yellow Calla Lilies, which still brightens my kitchen up nicely. A few days later, she brought her husband, Richard, to meet me. Richard is an Englishman, and a caring man, who just created and printed a fine list of people living on this street, complete with names, phone numbers, addresses, and e-mail addresses. And there I am at the top of his list, because I own the first home on the street. What a joy to know Margaret and Richard!

When my patio furniture arrived in two huge boxes, I knew I was in trouble. Can't get down on my knees anymore, and this was a "down on the knees" kind of job! On Mother's Day, my neighbors down the road,

Kathy and Joey, showed up with a tarp and worked for five hours (five hours!!!) putting the round table and four chairs together and giving me a chance to enjoy life outside in a whole new way. And then, Rick walked up the hill with a cane. I wondered if something bad had happened to Rick. Nope! He was here to give me an absolutely gorgeous hand-made wooden cane, light wood with dark running through it, that had been made by his wife "Mickey's" father. It's so beautiful that I can't bear to use it, and will be hanging it on a wall in the "Grandfather Room"—one of my two guest bedrooms. Rick, a well-known song writer in these parts, even wrote a song about me: "The Wizard of 101 Corner Oak Court."

My friend Warren comes by often to check up on me and to sit and chat for a while, with his fine Golden Retriever. Warren makes sure I know about events going on in the larger community that folks on our street are sure to attend. Always good to see him at my door. Mark and Betsy have become great friends too, and always review my writings for spelling and grammar (he was a high school English teacher). Anyone who reads my stuff and comments on it is a great friend in my book!

And then, just this week, I had taken the trash bin down the driveway to the street, when my legs started giving me trouble on the way back to the house. I almost fell. Jim and his fifteen-year-old daughter, Emma, were driving by just then, noticed my distress, and stopped. Emma grabbed the leash of the large part-Doberman girl I'm taking care of just now, and Jim grabbed me. With the help of both of those observant, friendly neighbors, we made it to the sliding glass door and into my living room! And then, to put the frosting on the cake, so to speak (my mother enjoyed that expression a lot), who shows up at my door the next day but Jim's wife, Sherry. She handed me a plastic container filled to the brim with homemade chicken noodle soup!! What a treat!!

The longer I am here, the more friends I meet. Not all of them are on this street, either. Caroline, a server in our clubhouse, always treats me and my friends and relatives extremely well, and greets me with a "Hi, Ace" whenever I show up. Alice, a guard at the North Gate, phones me every morning at 10:00 a.m. to make sure I'm all right. She does that because my son requested that service so that my family could be assured daily that I've made it through another night, but by this time she and I have become good friends and I stop at the guardhouse to say "Hello" in person once a week or so. There's Buddy Moss, head of security here in Lake Arrowhead, and a good friend of my son "Hawk" ever since they were a team of motorcycle cops down in Cobb County. Maybe it's my white hair. Maybe it's the cane. Maybe it's my stunning good looks. Maybe I've become a special project. Whatever it is, I have friendships here in Lake Arrowhead that I prize greatly. These people, these friends, are among the very best! Silver and Gold!

A Mother's Day Gift

On the Thursday before Mother's Day, three huge boxes appeared on my porch. The patio furniture had finally arrived: glass topped table, four fancy swivel chairs, a heavy base for the huge umbrella, and the huge umbrella itself. It had all been on "back order". I let the stuff sit there on the porch. I know my limitations! One box, the printed side told me, weighed 126.5 pounds. I sure wasn't going to move that!!

Thursday night, though, some critter had let curiosity get the better of it and tore open the boxes. No edibles. But I decided I'd better unpack those boxes and bring the contents inside, just in case the critter came back with mayhem on its mind. Took me an hour and filled my dining area with patio parts. Filled! Ugly wrappings still on all those parts. There were instructions. I read them. There was no way this old fella was going to put those parts together. No way! So, the patio parts just stayed there in the dining area, taking up space. The empty boxes just stayed on the porch.

Mother's Day dawned clear and cool. I cleaned up, dressed, grabbed my cane and bumped my way down the thirteen stairs to make my cup of coffee and send e-mail greetings to all the mothers in my extended family. There are a lot of them, and I finally got my breakfast at about 10:00 a.m. Then I took a break (hey, I'm no spring chicken!) and plunked myself down in my recliner to reminisce about my mother, a very special lady. I may have dozed a bit. I got a wake-up call right after most folks eat lunch. It was Joey and Kathy, neighbors way down the street. I'd met them once before. "We noticed a bunch of large boxes on your porch as we drove by this morning, and wonder if you need any help putting something together?" Out here in the North Georgia foothills, everything arrives in boxes and has to be put together. "We'll be over about 3:00 this afternoon, if that's OK." (It was sure OK!!) They came, put down a tarp on the patio, and began dragging all those patio parts out of the dining area, through the living room and out. As they worked, several other folks who live on Corner Oak Court came by, saw their car, and stopped in to help or to supervise. Joey and Kathy worked out there on my patio until almost 8:00! But then it was done!! I had a patio with patio furniture! And those empty boxes were gone too, out to my storage shed. Beautiful!

The deer, who are accustomed to having their dinner promptly at 5:30, were "hanging out" some distance away, murmuring deer curses at us. I filled their containers with quartered apples and field corn. Joey, Kathy, and I took one last close up look at the spectacular new patio and went inside to allow the deer (who are a bit "skittish" around people) to have their dinner. We sat in the living room, watching through the glass wall, and enjoying some cool white wine and a couple of Corona beers. Could I do anything for Joey and Kathy that would help me recover from my huge case of Norwegian Lutheran guilt? "Absolutely not! We've got to get home because we have some chicken marinating and it's past time for dinner." And my new friends and great neighbors left.

My entire day had been a Mother's Day gift. But I'm still not sure how to deal with the guilt.

Heroes

Have you noticed how much talk we hear these days about "heroes"? Every evening on the news, someone is featured performing a heroic act. Lately there have been way too many opportunities. Massive fires in our western states, disastrous hurricane damage and death in the deep South, Puerto Rico all but flattened by high winds and torrential rains. Heroes are created when Mother Earth turns on us, created sometimes out of people whose friends and neighbors would never have thought had the spirit of heroes.

I have never been a hero, except perhaps to my boys when they were growing up. Children look to their daddies for heroism, and even love can seem heroic to them. I've been in situations at times in my life when heroic action might have been required of me—in the Army in Europe facing Soviet armies just across the border, for example—but the need for heroism never materialized. I was never tested, in any conventional sense, to prove my heroism.

So, it's interesting to me that in just two weeks I will have been visited by two real life heroes, one at a time. Their names are Cris and Joe, and both have faced terrifying situations as heroes. Back in 1992, I was serving as the Acting Regional Health Administrator for the U.S. Public Health Service, responsible for a regional office that worked with eight Southern states. A part of that job was to support staff that handled emergency preparedness for health, and not many staff, either! Two full-time Commissioned Officers and a third officer who had special skills that could prove extremely valuable in a disaster. Cris spoke Spanish.

By mid-August 1992, we knew that Hurricane Andrew was going to strike the coast of Florida on or about August 24. We knew it was the strongest hurricane to hit Miami in thirty years, the third strongest in the entire United States in the 20th Century. And so, upon my orders, Joe and Cris went to Miami days ahead of the disaster to perform assessments, make arrangements for the health care of the population (roofs blew off hospitals, for example, but we were ready with fully staffed full field hospitals in tents that could be set up in less than a day and operate for 72 hours without any impact on the local economy, water, food, or power). The storm hit with 165 mile an hour winds, dropping about eight inches of rain on south Miami. The direct death toll rose to twenty-six with another forty deaths attributable to the hurricane, and those officers hung in there, right in the middle of it all, reporting back as fifty-nine health facilities were damaged or destroyed. Those men were and are heroes in every sense of the word.

Later, since I held temporarily the rank of a Rear-Admiral even as a civilian Public Health official, I flew over the damage in a military helicopter, identifying sites in need of our help and pin-pointing where we should focus our resources. Nothing heroic in that. I also identified a female Commissioned Officer on my staff to manage the follow-up efforts. She was there for six months! She, and several others who worked with me, were also clearly heroic in a time of real need.

They visit me because we worked together in a time of great crisis, and they still see me as a friend and leader. I am honored and proud to be visited by these heroic Commissioned Officers.

It Was One Of Those Family Days!

On Saturday, my youngest son, "Hawk" (his Norwegian real name is "Haakon") arrived at the cabin promptly at 8:00 a.m. and carried three heavy boxes, each containing a small bookcase, upstairs for me. Then we were off in the rain, driving to Athens, Georgia to check out my oldest son's new home. All three of my boys are back in Georgia now, and so am I. Nice how that worked out. There are probably more folks named "Hagebak" in Georgia today than there are in Minnesota!!

"Hawk" was looking for a "biscuit place" along the way—the sort of thing you find every couple of miles in Georgia, a place that serves "sawmill gravy" on the top of your opened biscuit, and you think you must have died and wound up, in heaven! We drove two and a half hours and saw nary a one of those places. Finally, breakfast in a little Mexican restaurant on the outskirts of Athens. Not a biscuit in sight!

Beaumont shares his new digs with a blind dog ancient of days, and his mom (my first wife) who is still younger than I am. Toured his home (he overlooked the 50 cent tour fee) and marveled, particularly, at the finished basement, which has a room you could install a bowling alley in. We had a great family time, the four of us. Enough water has flowed over the dam to make it fairly easy for my first wife and me to communicate in a friendly manner. We had a great five hours there. Beaumont had whipped up some collard greens and offered them to us for lunch. We just couldn't eat another bite of anything, after that big breakfast in the Mexican restaurant. Thank whatever gods there may be for allowing us to refuse the collard greens without lying!

Then we were off to Jefferson, Georgia (sounds Colonial, doesn't it, but it's probably Confederate, named after Jefferson Davis, I don't know for sure) to visit granddaughter Savannah, her husband Nick, their son Jack who will be a big brother in a few months, granddaughter Stacie's husband Pete, who is a police dog trainer finishing up his work here and eager to return home to his wife and daughter in Germany. I spent some quality time with little Jack, just entering his "terrible twos". He had to explain every photo in a family photo album, telling me who everyone was in those pictures. Longest conversation I ever had with Jack, and it was great fun, although I'm not at all sure that he understood what I was saying and I certainly didn't understand what he was telling me. The important thing, really, is listening. That's *always* the important thing.

Still raining all the way back to the cabin, and I was pleased to leave the driving to "Hawk". Car headlights in the rain don't seem to affect him the way they affect me. Wonder why? Got home at 8:00 p.m., exhausted but with warm feelings about the joy that being with family brings.

To bed early, planning to sleep long and well. At 3:15 a.m., though, the power went out all over Lake Arrowhead and my CPAP breathing machine was slowly smothering me. Got up, had half a glass of red wine, and fell asleep in my chair with the cat on my lap. The lights came on at 6:30, and I trotted back up to bed. Today I put together three bookcases and emptied four of the twelve boxes of family photo albums. Now I'm ready to just sit and read. Great weekend, though!! I've been blessed. I'd do it all again in a minute, if it weren't for those collard greens!

An Early Morning Call

Up at the usual time, about 7:30 this morning, and was in my recliner with that morning cup of coffee when my phone rang. It was a Sunday, and early, and so I thought the worst. I'm always "parading the horribles".

Somehow, the terrible things my mind can visualize are far worse than reality. Does that happen to you, too? I guess it's Mother Nature's way of preparing us for bad stuff, maybe.

My eldest son was on the line from Athens, Georgia, home of the gigantic University of Georgia, and now his home once again as well. He wanted me to know that my youngest son, "Hawk", and his wife Lisa had driven all the way to Athens on Saturday to help him get settled into his newly purchased home. I sent an e-mail to my youngest son this morning, thanking him for helping his disabled oldest brother. He said in return, "Those of us who can help, must help."

It's hard to explain, even to myself, the joy I feel that all three of my sons are now close to me again. But then I remembered my father's face when I walked up the steps to the front door of our home in Blue Earth, Minnesota, and he came to the door to meet me. I was finally home from the Army, still in uniform of course, having served two years in the forces occupying Germany after World War II. That time was known as the "Cold War", and we few stationed there were a thin line of defense against a feared major attack by Russian forces. In the United States, school children were still hiding under desks in a vain attempt at being safe from bombing. My father opened the door and reached out to hold me in his arms. There was so much love in his face at that moment that it was all I could do to remain standing. I really had never understood, until that very moment, how much I meant to that father of mine.

These three sons mean the same to me. And now, through what may have seemed ill fortune as divorces split families apart, mine and his, all three of my sons are all back in Georgia, our adopted home. We were all born in the upper Midwest, but a chance meeting with a group of mental health professionals from Georgia at a conference in Chicago led me to join Governor Jimmy Carter's team to build, with the blessings of his wife Rosalyn, a network of mental health services across the State of Georgia. When I moved south to do that work, my family moved with me. Three sons, now back together. Perhaps each of them has an understanding of how much they mean to me, their father. I think they do.

Some early morning phone calls can be wonderful.

A Norwegian Historian Tracks The Family

Sometime in the early 1880's, a professional photographer, on his way to photograph a country wedding, stopped at the sod house owned by Beret Hagebak (1810—1903) to water his horse and probably himself as well. He took three photos of Beret. The most famous photo has appeared in many American history books and shows the lady seated in front of her "soddie", her cat, whose ears were frozen off during one of those Minnesota winters, sitting in the doorway. Another photo showed Beret with her clay pipe. She smoked it regularly, believing it would improve her health. The third photo was a portrait of the lady in her kerchief. She was no great beauty by any means, but she was one tough lady. She spent thirty of her ninety-three years living in that "...house made of dirt".

Her photos eventually made their way back to her home in Norway, where they were seen by a Norwegian author/historian, Hans Olav Lokkon. He visited the area where Beret had lived in Minnesota, met the one descendant still living there, toured the museum where her kerchief and other artifacts are preserved, and visited the Borgund Lutheran Church cemetery where she was buried near her husband and other members of her family. Hans Olav decided that hers was a story worth telling and contacted Floie Vane in Washington State to get more information. He also made contact with me. Together, Floie and I had written a family history/genealogy book in 2010.

And so it was that this morning, at Hans Olav's request, I wrote ten short stories, paragraphs really, about the lady who lived in the sod house—my great-great grandmother. They will appear in some form in a new book Hans Olav is writing about Norwegian pioneer families in the United States. He's also tracked down living relatives in Norway, to build a link between those who made the hazardous and long journey to western Minnesota in the 1860's and those who remained in the land of their birth.

My extended family, all "Hagebaks" but many by another name as the result of marriage, now numbers hundreds of direct descendants of Beret and her husband John. Most, but not all, know something of the history of their family. Documents were saved, so we can see when the family formally became citizens of the United States, or precisely which pieces of Minnesota land were homesteaded and eventually owned by them. Photographs of stern-faced people (getting your picture taken was serious business a few generations ago) with names written on the back, allow us to see those who went before. We're a family of collectors, I suppose, and that's not all bad. Cousin Floie has one of the sea chests that the emigrants brought with them from Norway.

I suppose that, for some people, knowing family history seems a bit silly. We Americans tend to be a forward-looking people, and what is past is past. But there are those of us whose identity is strengthened by an understanding of who came before, and what they had to deal with in order to survive and grow. Floie and I, and now Hans Olav Lokkon over in Norway, are part of this latter group. The study of ancestry has never been more popular than it is today, and documents defining your family can be found, sometimes in the strangest places. The stories of your family can be absolutely fascinating. I urge you to begin searching for them.

Cleaning Frenzy

I know it's kind of silly to be taking a "vacation" away from this place used by so many for their vacations. But this is more of a nostalgia trip than a vacation. No fancy hotels overlooking ocean beaches. This will be driving, lots of driving.

I'm going to western Minnesota so see my wonderful older cousin, the lady who responded when I said to her, "Y'know, if I had been ten years older I would have chased you around the block a few times", by saying, "And if I had been ten years younger, I would have run slow!" I love that lady. Then up to Fargo (it's summer so it's OK) to see my Queen, the Homecoming Queen in our Senior year in high school. I am her loyal subject and a Knight of the Realm. I'll have to put up with her husband and her twin brother, but the twin brother's lovely wife and the lady who is my Queen make that trip worthwhile! Then off to Grand Rapids, Minnesota, to visit a fellow "shrink" and his lovely wife. He's OK for a "shrink", but she's lovely! On to northern Wisconsin, Ashland to be exact, about 60 miles due east of Duluth, to visit Sandy—at one time the youngest Dean of Women in the United States. I happened to be the Dean at Northland College and hired her. Sandy fooled the experts on the old television show "What's My Line?" and even got her photo on the cover of *Parade Magazine*, back when it was a magazine. Today it's just a flyer tucked into your Sunday paper. Then down to Hutchinson, Minnesota to visit Cort and his wife Vi. Cort's an old high school buddy, smart as a whip and humorous too, and even lucky. He married Vi. On to the twin metropoli (metropolises?) Minneapolis and St. Paul, to see Pete, Sue, and Phil for dinner somewhere. And then, finally, to my "home town", Blue Earth, Minnesota, where I will spend time with old friends, visit my paid-for plot in the local cemetery, and take my once sweetheart (I started to say my "old high school girlfriend" and thought better of it) and her husband who was around when I wasn't thanks to the Army (he got out of the Army at about the time that I went in), but who I have come to like a great deal, and my dear friend Elaine, who does most all the real work for our high school class reunions, out to dinner. I'm just the M.C. She does the work. (Don't tell her.) Then "home again, home again, jiggity jig"!! Nostalgia. Where would we be without it??

And so…given all that…it was time to clean house today. Whenever my childhood family took a major trip, it was time to first clean the house. Mother taught me that. She taught me a lot of stuff, but that stuck. "Suppose something happened to us and people had to come into our house and look around?" she would say. My sister and I suffered many a sleepless night wondering about all the things that could happen to us. Uffda! And thus today I washed all of the shelves and bins in the old refrigerator I got with the cabin. And I took the stove apart and put those circular metal things that fit into the holes where the heating elements go in the stove into the dishwasher. I used Windex on the sinks and washed down the counter tops. The Kuerig coffee maker got a bit of a scrubbing. Went out and bought a battery-operated leaf blower to spare my new friends the embarrassment of having to walk past my leaf-strewn driveway. Kind of fun using it, actually. Appeals to the macho in me. (Not much of that to go around these days, now that I'm eighty). Watered the plants. Dusted. Vacuumed. I was going to hang the bedding out on the clotheslines but realized I didn't have clotheslines. Trash into the trashcan outdoors. Repaired the porcelain figurine of an old sailor showing a ship model to a young boy. The move across country had knocked off the old sailor's hand with the ship model, so it looks as though he is talking with the boy about how pirates cut off his hand. If the super glue doesn't hold, that's going to become the story. I paid bills. Got birthday cards for folks having birthdays while I'm away (why are so many of us born in June?) Listed all the things I would need to take on the trip. Began a "staging area" for all that stuff. Didn't do the filing because it bores me to tears, and I'll just leave that up to those people who are going to come into my house and look around if anything bad happens to me on the trip.

Oh, and I hired a cleaning lady. She starts the week I get back from "vacation".

Coming Home Again!

Vacations are fine things, even when you're eighty-plus and long retired from the world of work. Mine this year was a trip to the Upper Midwest of my youth, a nostalgia trip to Minnesota, North Dakota, and far northern Wisconsin. Over 1,500 miles were put on a new rental car, which took me to see old friends and even to meet a few new friends along the way. The Southwest Airlines flight back to Georgia was half an hour *early*—unheard of!—my own car started right up as it should, and my log cabin was waiting for me when I pulled into the driveway at 9:30 p.m., my usual bedtime. Family had hung balloons welcoming me home, and there was a "Hungry Man" dinner in the freezer! I sat up a while, remembering.

The following day was absolutely astounding! The sun shone brightly all day, the afternoon temperature hovered at around 79 degrees, and there was *no humidity*!! Yet it's near the end of June, in Georgia!! Clothes were washed, groceries were bought and put away, and bills were paid by early afternoon. The patio umbrella was raised and the glass table beneath it was cleaned. The patio itself was dappled with sunlight and leafy shadows. The hummers and the birds had found their fresh food, and a squirrel was nibbling at the old birdseed I'd dumped. Life had returned to my old log home in the woods.

There were still chores to do, of course. But they could wait. I sat there beneath the umbrella and watched the world go by. Friends stopped to welcome me home. Then, just as I was about to go inside to deal with a thousand little tasks, I spotted a dark black fuzzy caterpillar making its way across the patio, ever so slowly, ever so purposeful. The tasks at hand waited while I watched the caterpillar inch along. Would it become one of those large black butterflies with the blue lining in its wings? I hoped so. After crossing this patio, it deserved to become very special.

One of the great joys of life, I think, is to be able to put tasks aside on the first day home again and watch a caterpillar instead. It's my hope that you can take time to watch a caterpillar, too, on a day as gorgeous as this one was, at a home that you love and have just returned to.

Me, The Party Planner!

I used to throw big lavish parties at the drop of a hat. My wife's birthday was on New Year's Eve, which made it easy to remember and led to some fun get-togethers with friends. (I usually asked that attendees bring some silly, low cost gift that would have meaning to her. Once an employee brought a spectacular multi-colored angel with wonderful wings—unreal!) There were "Syttende Mai" parties to celebrate Norwegian Independence Day and the table was heavy with such things as lefse, flatbrod, sardines, Aquavit, Swedish meatballs, assorted Scandinavian cheeses and meats—you get the picture. There were smaller coming-togethers with close friends and family, for the holidays. Always Thanksgiving was a big favorite. And always, I had the help of beautiful ladies to whom I was married—sequentially, of course.

Well, now I am single except for the cat, who got a bit excited when I mentioned "sardines" in the preceding paragraph. But she's not much help in party preparations. I'm on my own.

My very fine friends from California, Sharon and Brian, are coming on Tuesday. As my granddaughters say, "OMG"! I went out and bought some decent towel and washcloth sets. But there's more to a party than towels and washcloths. So, I invited about a dozen people or so from my new neighborhood. If the thought of a dozen new friends descending on your log cabin doesn't motivate you to get your party act together, nothing will. I want my California friends to meet my new Georgia friends and neighbors who have been so darned good to me. And I want them all to enjoy the experience.

So…beer, white wine, red wine…what else? Oh, shrimp. And assorted cheeses, and equally assorted meats, and a fine assortment of fruits in nibble sizes, and chips and dip, and crackers, mixed nuts (in addition to my friends.) ☺ (Sorry, couldn't resist!) Soft drinks and water for the faint of heart. Maybe some flowers for a centerpiece? Oh, and bowls and stuff. How did she wind up with all the bowls in the divorce settlement? What was I thinking? And tubs, and ice. Napkins, paper plates and cups, all color coordinated!

The downtown merchants greet me by name these days. Big smiles. I am loved.

My cleaning lady agreed to come Monday morning. I'll blow the leaves off the driveway and patio on Monday with my new leaf blower. I'm feeding the deer a bit right now, telling myself that it's between the berries and the acorns (Spring and Fall) so they must be hungry. I want my California friends to go back home marveling at the wildlife. Heck, I may even toss out a steak (dang the cost!) to give the Californian's a chance to meet my bear.

I'm busy as a one-armed paper hanger (another of my mother's little sayings) but I'm so excited to see my California friends again, share them with my new neighbors, and hold a real open house. I even cleaned my closet!!! (Think not? You should have seen it last week!)

The Party's Over ...

In the words of the immortal Nat King Cole, the party's over—and so is the clean-up. And it was all just great! My first real party in this old log cabin has come and gone, as have my first visitors from an earlier life, my friends from California, Brian and Sharon. I was ready for them, with foods, and wines, and two guest bedrooms to choose from. I wasn't ready for them emotionally though, and so I cried as they came through my door with hugs for this old mountain man. I'm a Norwegian, and Norwegians are known for their stoicism. But when faced with people who love me, I'm just a puddle of mush. Some Viking I would have made!

My friends who live on Corner Oak Court began arriving at 2:30 p.m. It wasn't long before every chair in the place was taken except for the ancient and frail small antique chair that held a sign created special for the day, saying: "This chair is older than dirt. Please don't try to sit on it!" Brian and Sharon met everyone, and everyone met Brian and Sharon. And for several hours we all enjoyed one another's company—and some shrimp, cheeses, meats, fruit, candies, wines, beers, water, and soft drinks. Nobody left hungry, but there was a small mountain of foods and drinks left over. I'll freeze the food, except for the fruit, and warned folks that they would likely see the shrimp, cheeses and meats again sometime. (And they will.) Friends and family won't let the beer and wine go stale.

Because this was to be an "open house" with even a clean closet in the "Master Suite" (pretty snooty for a log cabin, isn't it!?) I gave little mini-tours of the place—thirteen steps up, thirteen steps down, so I got some exercise. Many of my guests had never been inside the cabin, though they had lived on Corner Oak Court for years, and they all seemed impressed by the fact that the inside of the cabin seems somehow larger than the outside. At least they commented on the size. Some were amazed that a single guy could manage to have a clean home. (My friendly cleaning lady did come the day before, but I saw no reason to mention that!) And

Sharon thought that I should have been an interior decorator. Wow! But I did OK as a psychologist. The jobs are similar in some ways. (What the heck did he mean by *that?*)

I think that the truly grand thing about this party wasn't the food and drink, or even the mini-tours. It was the fact that people with very different backgrounds and life experiences, coming together from Georgia and from California, could find common ground to share stories and bits of themselves with one another in an old log cabin on a Tuesday afternoon. These are my friends. They expect nothing less of themselves, or of me, or of others, really. And I love them all.

Brian and Sharon and I talked into the night, as friends who have not seen one another in a long time will do. In the morning, after breakfast, while they were preparing to leave for Charlotte to spend a day or two with their son before flying back home to California, the miracle I had been hoping for happened, and five or six grown and half-grown deer, and one little fawn still sporting spots, showed up in the yard. Pictures were taken, and that little fawn is going to wind up on Facebook!! The perfect ending to a perfect time with my friends — those who live down the street, and those who live all the way out in California. I am so blessed!!

So Today There's A Spring In My Step!

Yesterday I stopped at the Home Depot to pick up a full propane tank for this fine old grill I somehow inherited from the lady who owned this cabin in the woods before me. The Courtesy Counter was right there near the door, and a cheerful lady of indeterminate age went out of her way to welcome me to the store and ask how I was doing on this fine day. I gave her my stock line: "Pretty good, considering my age and general condition." She grinned and asked, "Well, how old are you?" "Eighty-one", I replied. "Nah", she said, "you're not anywhere near eighty-one." When I again told her my age, she said, "I sure hope that when I turn eighty-one, I'll be as spry and cheerful as you are!" As I checked out her rings (yep, married dammit!) I said, "There should be at least 6,000 copies of you in every store in the county, because you have a way of making a person feel just great!" She smiled. She ran my credit card, gave it back, and went outside to get my propane tank and load it into the car for me. What a lady!

I told my friend, James, about that experience over a glass of wine that evening, which led us to talk a bit about the great ladies in our lives. That must have been the cause of the dreams I had last night. That conversation, the wine, and the Home Depot lady. I dreamed all night of the ladies in my life, and it was wonderful. Not sexy or anything—I'm out of the running on that stuff—but just dreams about beautiful and talented women who have meant something to me over my many years.

I saw my mother again, younger again, one of the greatest, funniest, happiest people I have known. And I saw my sister, struggling with Multiple Sclerosis but maintaining a positive outlook on life right up to the time she died at age seventy-five. There were grade school crushes, young girls moving through my mind, and my high school sweetheart (I still love that seventeen-year-old girl, and even find that while love has flown for the adult version, I still like the person she has become, and her husband, too). Army days, and a young lady in Switzerland who spoke three languages, none of them English, but friends translated our letters to each other and I spoke a bit of "soldat Deutsch" (soldier German, spoken poorly) whenever we got together. I was too young to marry, but I might have married that girl if I hadn't been so homesick. My first wife, mother of our three sons, an Iowa farm girl, showed up in the dreams. So did a secretary of mine who was married when I was single, and single when I was married. Great timing! And my beautiful second wife, my wife for forty years of wonderful memories—traveling, sailing, raising boys, welcoming grandchildren, and so much more—she was there in the dreams as well. I even dreamed of my Queen, living now with her husband far away, a talented, caring woman now who has been my friend since third grade. A wonderful night's sleep filled with dreams of delightful women who have meant so much to me over the years.

And so today, thanks to a chance meeting with a cheerful lady in a Home Depot store, I am walking with a spring in my step, and a song in my heart. Yesterday and last night led me to take stock of my life. I have known great affection, and I am a better person for it. I wish the same for you, and once in a while a night of sweet dreaming.

The Death Of A Friend ...

There was this guy I used to work with, long ages ago. I haven't seen him in years. He was a counselor who became a manager, then the Director of a non-profit community agency that served developmentally disabled people of all ages. He was as country as they come with a heart of pure gold. He cared about the people he worked to help. He now lived in Canton, Georgia, only twelve miles or so from my cabin. I didn't know that for the longest time.

We'd kept in touch over the years with Christmas cards, mostly, since my work with the U.S. Public Health Service took me away from the folks I had known in previous work settings. We didn't see one another for quite a few years before I moved to California, and when I did that, even the cards stopped.

Back in Georgia and divorced, I began looking up old friends. Found him down in Canton, and sent him a card saying, "Hey, we're neighbors now!" He got the card and phoned me last week. He was divorced, too. What's more, he was in a special "rehabilitation hospital" he called it. We talked half an hour or so. I never could get a clear answer about what the heck was wrong with him. I offered to come down and see him.

He tricked me then. He was getting out of the hospital the next day, he said, and would be heading home. "Well, I'll visit you there". He told me to wait a week or so because he had some things to do around the place before he could welcome visitors. One of those things, apparently, was to die.

His ex-wife contacted me yesterday to tell me that he had passed away that morning. He'd made a short list of people he wanted her to contact and my name was on it. The funeral was going to be this Saturday, at 2:00 p.m. "Can you be there? He would have wanted you to visit and meet his kids." "I'll be there." Thinking to myself that his ex must be quite a lady to be taking on this responsibility even though the marriage had gone sour. But human caring is a powerful motivator, even in the worst of circumstances (or maybe because of those circumstances). She gave me her phone number, saying that her home was "headquarters" for people coping with my friend's death. Where else? Who else? Of course her home was "headquarters".

I expect the chapel to be packed with developmentally disabled people from all over this part of Georgia. I may even see once more, other old friends who shared their working lives with me so many years ago. I will meet his two grown children and tell them that I always thought their dad was one heck of a guy. And I will probably cry. If a man can't cry at a funeral, when can he cry?

He was seventy-six. He's used most of those years to make a difference for people unable to help themselves. The world and I are going to miss him.

A Most Interesting Funeral

I grew up in a fertile valley town in the upper Midwest, a Norwegian Lutheran boy with all the baggage that carries with it. Funerals there were somber events as befitting the stoic Norwegians of my childhood. The music was muted, typically sung by a soloist. There was often a eulogy written and recited by a family member. The minister's remarks were brief, focused on reminding us of our own mortality as the embalmed body of a friend or relative served to illustrate the point. There was a luncheon served by the Ladies Aid in the church basement after the services.

Yesterday I attended my very first funeral in the South. A friend and co-worker had died two days earlier and knowing that he was about to die he'd spent some of his last hours contacting people he cared for by phone. He had called me, just to renew our friendship. He had also spoken with a black minister who was a friend of his, to express his final wishes for how his funeral was to be conducted. My friend was Caucasian. He had spent most of his life as a behavioral counselor and as a manager of others, working primarily with developmentally disabled children and adults, white and black. He was something of a pioneer in that regard, helping to bring racial harmony to communities in the deep South through his own caring manner.

And so, it was no real surprise to me that following my friend's casket into the funeral home chapel was a black preacher and a black choir of twelve powerful voices. Those seated in the pews were ninety-five per cent white. After the family was seated, the choir sang two songs of praise, "happy songs", just as my friend had requested. Then a white preacher stepped up, kneeled next to a front pew, and began to pray—beginning softly, but then raising his voice to a shout, a crescendo of sound, praising his Lord and the deceased. The choir again moved forward to sing two more songs, accompanied by clapping hands beating time to the music, first by choir members, and then by some of the friends and family in the audience. It became a joyful sound.

The black preacher then took the podium to tell us that my friend had asked him to be brief. He pointed out that some funeral services were three hours in length, but that he would be brief and hoped that those attending wouldn't feel cheated. He then spoke for thirty or forty minutes, bringing into his lively remarks Moses, Noah and the flood, Jesus Christ, God, and my friend. He closed with a prayer, my friend's body was removed, and we were ushered out.

My friend had made his point once again, working to improve racial harmony in a less than harmonious world. It was his last statement, and it was powerful and effective. I don't know when I have been more proud of a friend and colleague as I was yesterday. It was a funeral I will always remember—my very first funeral in the South.

New Year's Eve At The Cabin

I'm alone here at the cabin tonight, but my cat, "Putih", is with me. She's asleep on the sofa (I used to call it a "davenport" but got so many chuckles from the grandchildren that I had to switch), so she'll not be helping me stay up until midnight. And a New Year is about to begin.

Sixty-three years ago tonight, there was a New Year about to begin, too. I was in the U.S. Army, and got home for a few days to celebrate Christmas with my mom and dad, my kid sister, and my beautiful girlfriend. I wanted to stay, basking in the warmth of familiar faces and places, but that is not the Army way. On December 28, I boarded a train to head back to Fort Leonard Wood, Missouri, and an unknown future. Within a day I was in New Jersey, preparing to ship out for Germany, where I would become part of the post-World War II occupation.

And then, as luck would have it, I did not draw KP duty, or guard duty, or any other duty either, and was given a three-day pass!! So did five other guys. We got together, boarded another train, and headed into New York City for New Year's Eve on Time's Square. Found a hotel willing to take on six soldiers in one room. I drew the large overstuffed chair. Four guys drew the bed, sleeping sideways. Another guy had to sleep on the floor. And then we went out into the night.

I headed for Time's Square, where the action was. I was always interested in where the action was. There I was, right in the middle of it all, a pushing, shoving crowd waiting for the ball to drop, and standing next to an old fellow dressed as Father Time. And then the crowd shoved his wife and daughter out of the way, separating the family of Father Time. What the heck? I was in uniform, in the best physical condition of my young life, and I began shoving back. Nobody would mess with a soldier in uniform. Within minutes, I had the family back together again.

"Stand by me," said Father Time, "and you'll be on television." A reward, of sorts. I stood by him. The globe dropped. And way back in Minnesota, my mom and dad saw me on television! I'll never forget it.

Tonight, I'm sixty-three years older. The television set shows a Time's Square I don't recognize. My mom and dad have both gone to their reward, as has my sister. My girlfriend is a grandmother, happily married to a fine man that I consider to be a friend of mine. The camp I was assigned to in New Jersey has been closed for years. My Army home in Germany is now a place where diplomats from all over the world come to relax and communicate, guarded by German troops. I know. I tried to go there to relive that life a couple of years ago and couldn't get past the front gate.

Each year, though, I celebrate New Year's Eve in New York City's Time's Square, in my memory. I don't need to leave the cabin. Time's Square, my mom, dad, sister, and girlfriend are just as real as if they were here with me. Happy New Year to you, too. A very Happy New Year. With love.

4. Some Thoughts Of A Man Living Alone

Living alone gives a person a good bit of time for just plain old thinking. These are a few of the thoughts that an old, single now, fellow had from time to time as he sat in his recliner with a good book and a glass of wine. The stories talk of being alone, of some admittedly "dumb stuff" to think on, and of important things like love and marriage, anger, sadness, and other musings often of an emotional type.

Being Alone

Talking with a friend the other evening about living alone, I was overcome with the sudden realization that I had never, ever, in my whole life, really been alone before. From birth up through high school my parents and kid sister had been such a deep part of my life that I never gave loneliness a thought. Truth be told, I never gave much of anything a thought.

That high school graduation summer I left for the Army. The Army is not a job that caters much to being alone. Cots, sometimes bunk bed cots, two-person pup tents, bathrooms with gang showers and no partitions anywhere—you're never alone in the Army. Army to college then, after a month at home with my folks, to share a two-person dorm room with two other guys and Army-style bunk beds again. Crowded. Thankfully those two guys were veterans like myself, who knew the dance of living with others in close quarters.

Then a first marriage and seventeen years of togetherness with my wife and, eventually, with three sons. A divorce, but the boys continued to live with me and ate "Hamburger Helper" every day of the week (to hear them tell it!). Another marriage, two adults and a gaggle of boys (hers and mine) in a two-bedroom condo that we sold as quickly as possible. Forty years, give or take a month or two, of being together in all sorts of communities—some good, some great—but always together. And then another divorce, and quite suddenly I was alone. Really alone.

This old log cabin had been vacant for a while, and the cabin and I made quite a pair. It sits, alone, on a high piece of ground in a rock-strewn half acre, with no other homes in sight. I wake up alone each morning in my old log cabin. Family and friends visit, and I relish their company. They helped me settle more gracefully than I ever could have on my own, making small repairs and always praising the cabin as "cozy" or "comfortable", or even as "beautiful". New neighbors have brought me flowers, a righteously rich cherry pie, a huge and delicious quiche. They have stopped by to fix things as we became friends, one couple put together a whole patio set, others hauled empty boxes to the shed, shared a glass of wine and some cheese perhaps, invited me to parties and community events, always making me feel welcome and wanted here. Those friends and relatives chip away at the "alone" in my life. They always help.

One friend suggested that living alone may not be such a bad thing after all. There's nobody to tell you where to put this or that, nobody to insist that the sheets need washing *today*, no argument over which television show to watch or when to eat, sleep, or get the mail. He was right, of course. Being alone fosters independence and decision-making skills. Being alone can be handled. But that huge old stuffed bear and the two little ones sharing the couch across from my recliner just don't seem to fill the need for closeness that I seem to relish. (I do talk to the bears, though)

Some Things I Have Noticed About Living Alone

Living alone is a mixed blessing, as anyone who has ever done it for any length of time will most certainly tell you. Here are a few of the mixed "blessings" I've begun to notice after six months.

- Most things sold in grocery stores are created for two or more people. I have stuff in my freezer that I no longer recognize, but at least it's not moving.
- If I roll over in bed, nobody is in danger of being crushed. (The cat sleeps downstairs).
- Supper (I'm a country boy, so that's what I call it!) doesn't taste the same, somehow. And there are no pleasant surprises. You know what you've cooked. No surprises at all.
- If you get caught up in an early morning project of some kind, nobody minds if you have breakfast at noon.
- You stay in the house when the cleaning lady makes her monthly visit, just to have someone to talk to. Talking to yourself gets old fast and can be kind of scary.
- You can, and probably do, lead a rich fantasy life.
- Shaving every day seems kind of silly. But you do it, because you never know.

- The raspberries, strawberries, and big blueberries go bad before you've eaten half of them. The boxes are too big. And the contents don't freeze well. DO NOT TRY THIS AT HOME.
- You wake up in the morning, visit the little room, and can—if you wish—go right back to bed. But there is a little inner voice that sounds like your mother and makes you get dressed instead.
- The same shirt can be worn for several days, unless you have a doctor's appointment. Then you must wear a clean shirt. Doctor's look for such things. Not just sure why.
- You don't go out to a restaurant very often if you're alone, because somehow that's more unpleasant than cooking your own meal at home. People look at you funny. And servers seat you by the kitchen or the bathrooms at a table that's too small to hold what you ordered because they know they aren't going to get the same tip as a table of sixteen.

But visits from good friends and caring relatives are such a huge blessing when you live alone. You have a shot at really knowing what caring and friendship are all about. Really! Outstanding!

Life Is Change, I Guess

Goodness knows, there have been some changes in my life these past few months. There probably have been in yours as well. Change is the "name of the game" for the living. For me, leaving a pristine (mostly) newly constructed home in a California suburb with an almost desert-like environment to come to an old log cabin in North Georgia with serious humidity and "critters" a lot more wild than the long-eared rabbits I'd been amused by in my California neighborhood was a sea-change of huge proportions. So was being single and alone.

Today, just because I could, I drove up to Blue Ridge, Georgia, a little town nestled in taller mountains about an hour's drive from my log cabin. We'd had a weekend log cabin of our own design up there fifteen or twenty years ago (I lose count, can barely even tell you *my* age, much less the age of that place), that we retired to and created the first chocolate shop in town, which we called "The Chocolate Express". Friends ran the bookstore up the street, serving coffee in the mornings to a bunch of us old fogies who lingered to tell stories of past lives and times. Another friend owned a rustic furniture store across the Main Street. A couple of gay guys, good friends, had a strange little restaurant crammed in between a couple of other buildings. Blue Ridge, Georgia was a fun place to visit, and a bit of a "tourist trap". Maybe more than "a bit".

I didn't go up the mountain road to see where our home had been. I'd heard that it had burned to the ground in a fire caused by a renter after we'd sold it. That change would have been way too much for me. But I did notice that every mile or two there were signs pointing the way to this vineyard or that vineyard. Mercy! I drove into town, recognized most of the buildings, but few of the shop signs. The old gas station where the old local guys used to sit and feed wild chickens and roosters was now a bicycle shop! No old guys. Just a few guys in "Spandex" with tight little bottoms. The bookstore was now a store that sold books, not coffee. Nobody sitting around telling tales. The furniture store hadn't changed, but the owner had. He didn't even recognize me. (Maybe I had changed some, too.) The little restaurant had been expanded, as had the menu, and the whole place was run by a little old lady who made sure I signed my VISA receipt.

"The Chocolate Express" was still using the name we had given it, and someone had installed an electric train high above the main room a foot from the ceiling, which ran at the flip of a switch to entertain children. The old glass cases were still used to display the chocolates, and the proprietors still carried the largest display of sugar free high-quality chocolates in all of Georgia. The owners had been there for nine years and loved the place. I left with a warm and fuzzy feeling, but without any chocolates (I'm dieting). They have expanded our shop, and it's good!

I'm not going to philosophize about change today. I just want you to know that I have seen it, and in some ways it's an improvement. It's all in how you view it. You sure can't escape it.

The Siren Song Of Books

There's a small library of books, two tall bookcases full, in the living room of this old log cabin. There's also a fairly large collection of what we used to call "pocket books" and eighty-five photo albums of pictures taken over the past forty years, upstairs. I love books. I've got most of what Stephen King, master of horror, ever wrote; a lot of Dean Koontz, Tom Clancy, and John Grisham; but also some real stuff like *The Illustrated Guide to Gardening*, *Theodore Rex*, Tom Brokaw's work on *The Greatest Generation*, *North American Birds*, and a lot of table top books on the Vikings. I keep Kahlil Gibran's *The Prophet*, on the table next to my chair and refer to it as some folks refer to the *Bible*, although I do have a special copy of the *Bible*, too. One whole shelf is devoted to my own writings, mostly about family or psychology. As I said, I love books.

In an old log cabin like this one, there are many things to be done just to manage the usual chores of daily living. There's a sign in my kitchen that shouts at me: "Real Vikings do dishes!", and I do dishes. Meals must be prepared, beds made, the carpet vacuumed, the cat fed and watered. I enjoy writing (obviously) and doing watercolor portraits of people and of animals. I've been working on a big old buffalo struggling through the snow for quite a while now. But my books call out to me: "Hey, sit down, pour yourself a glass of wine, and read." In the late afternoon and early evening, I give in to their siren song, select an old favorite, and do precisely that. But not until then.

You see, I usually feel guilty about reading when I "should" be doing something more productive. That old Norwegian Lutheran guilt is a tough thing to beat back, even when you're no longer a Lutheran. It's particularly difficult to deal with if the book you are reading is fiction—and you're reading for the simple pleasure of it. Pleasure is the cause of a whole lot of Norwegian Lutheran guilt. Trust me on that. Pleasure is sin's handmaiden. And when it's Stephen King that you're reading, you're well on your way to going to hell in a handbag. "Work for the night is coming!", is an old song learned as a child, and you just know that "night" is the big sleep, not the eight-hour variety! And Stephen King isn't helping!

So most mornings around this old cabin you'll find me working my tail off (look closely, no tail!) to be sure the bills are paid, the place is company clean, the cat is happy, and there are groceries in the refrigerator. It's the time that I write or paint, seldom preparing breakfast until 11:00 a.m. or later. Lists are made of chores to be done tomorrow, and all sorts of compulsive behaviors I learned as a child are in full sway. Afternoon may not get here until 2:00 p.m., or maybe even 3:00 p.m. When it finally comes, though, I grab a book and quite probably a glass of wine and plunk myself down in my recliner to read.

I have worked hard enough to beat back my guilt for another day. I have given myself over to the siren song of books. Why, heck! I might even watch some television if there's something good on—but I prefer books, and letting my brain make the pictures I see. It's my pleasure.

Beaumont R. Hagebak

Ya Gotta Have Contrasts

Our post office here in the Lake Arrowhead community is more of a mail pick-up point. It's outside, not too far from the north entrance, with a partial roof and a whole bunch of mailbox things making a wall. There are also large mailbox things for packages. I go there almost every day to get my mail at good old box number (Oh, lordy, I forgot—but it's right next to the box that somebody put an American flag decal on, so I can easily find it every time. Why bother to memorize a bunch of numbers? My theory is that my brain can only hold so much stuff, and if I don't have to cram more stuff into it, I won't lose so much falling out either). This outdoor mailroom sort of functions as a gathering place for we who live here. We always greet one another, even if we don't have a clue who we're greeting, because we're all in the mountain living thing together, I guess. Sometimes there's a joke, but always there's a comment on the weather.

Today was a gorgeous fall day at Lake Arrowhead. Sunny, a bit on the cool side, but not so you'd have to wear a jacket. Another fellow, a kid, I'd guess him to be no more than sixty-five, parked his car as I parked mine, and we both strolled up the path to pick up whatever was in our boxes. I commented, "Sure is a beautiful day," and then I went on to say, "I could enjoy it if every day were like this one." And then he said, "Well, ya gotta have contrasts. How would you come to appreciate a day like this one unless you had some bad days to compare it to?" And I thought, "Y'know, that's pretty darn profound." Told him so. He waved and drove off.

I don't like bad days. Heck, I don't like bad anything. That's why I love living up here in these North Georgia mountains. Oh, the squirrels annoy me sometimes when they attack the bird feeder, but right now they are "livin' in high cotton" or, to be more accurate, in a whole lot of acorns, and they don't bother my feeder at all. Not at all. The big old black bear had the potential for ruining my day, but as soon as I stepped out of the cabin and hollered at him, he ran off. That was a dumb move on my part, but it turned out to be a good bear-free day. The squirrels are gone for now, and that's a contrast from a month or two ago. The bear is gone too, back to its own lair, and that's a contrast for all of us who were a little rattled by him. But those are just simple contrasts.

The huge contrasts are fascinating if you look at them through the eyes of the fellow, I met today at the outdoor mail room. I find myself comparing my life alone with the life I had to leave back last February. I compare and contrast my old log cabin here with that brand-new home in California. New friends are contrasted with friends known for ages (still friends, though), and neither comes up short. The same with lovely ladies I have known and those I am learning to know at a very different age. I contrast health and energy at eighty-one with those aspects of my life at age thirty-one. All my days, and I dare to guess all of your days, too, are filled with contrasts. As the man said, "Ya gotta have contrasts."

Good, bad? Those decisions I leave up to you. But I am learning that life is full of contrasts, and perhaps that's precisely what makes it so very, very interesting. It is, you know.

Motivation

Got up this morning at 7:30 a.m., just like every other day, sort of wishing I could sleep in another half an hour. There weren't any odd noises in this cabin the whole night long, and I slept better than a baby. Babies wake up frequently. I was up only twice last night. So why did I get up at 7:30 this morning? Motivation. Plain and simple, motivation. I had a cat and some birds to feed. Nobody else was going to do it if I didn't. The cat still doesn't dare climb the stairs to my bedroom, and the birds can't get in the cabin anymore, I've seen to that. So if I hadn't been motivated

I could have stayed right there in my comfy, cozy bed. But, as all but a few (hopefully) negative and nasty people who know me will tell you, I am a decent guy and really want to take care of those I've taken on some responsibility for. "He's motivated", they will say. (Some will say, "He's crazy," but I am a psychologist and so I will be the best judge of that!)

People I know well, friends and relatives, will sometimes ask me, "Why do you write stuff, and why do you do watercolor paintings of people?" I do spend my days in the cabin writing "stuff" and painting portraits and petting the cat who sort of insists on that every hour or two. I usually give them some sort of fake answer: "Keeps me out of the bars and off the streets," or "Because otherwise I'd have to vacuum the cabin," or "I'm trying to make my first fortune at age eighty-one." The truth of the matter is, I'm motivated by immortality.

When I pass into the Great Beyond, I would like to be remembered, or at least thought of, once in a while. Half of my ashes, as some of you know, will be scattered beneath a fine tree so that I can live through nourishing that tree. The other half will be shipped to Blue Earth, Minnesota, to be buried in a plot I already own near a corn or soybean field across the dirt road from the cemetery. One year it's corn, the next it's soybeans. And my marker, supplied by the U.S. Veteran's Administration, will be quite simple. It will only say my full name, (no "Doctor"), date of birth and death, followed by "Sergeant, U.S. Army Europe, Garmisch Detachment". At the base it will say, "He loved his family, his friends, and his hometown." Not much there, really, to tell the passerby about this fellow who grew up in a small Minnesota town, loved and was loved by a passel of children and friends and by several wonderful ladies, descended from Norwegian Vikings and was oddly proud of that fact, had three sons and five delightful granddaughters, and a growing bunch of great-grandkids, and wound up in a log cabin in the North Georgia mountains. Oh, and he could paint portraits. And he was a writing fool.

So I am motivated to paint and write, and find that living alone allows me to do that easily, on whatever schedule I want once the cat is fed. That's the only real plus side to this living alone stuff. My fondest wish is that one day in the dim future, some great-great grandchild will take something I have written to "Show and Tell" in the third grade, or someone else's great-great grandchild will look at a painting I did years earlier, and ask, "Who is that and who did that painting?" And a mother or father somewhere will say, "Well, let's look on the back and see." And on the back will be the name of the subject, and my name, too. Immortality!

Thinking About Character

It's Sunday morning. Rain has been falling softly all night long. This old cabin's roof is made of shingles nailed over knotty pine boards, with no insulation in between — meaning, of course, that raindrops can be heard tapping on my roof no matter where I am in the cabin. The best spot for hearing raindrops is probably in my upstairs bedroom, although having my Sunday morning coffee in the living room, scrunched down in my leather recliner, two and a half stories straight down from the roof above, I can still hear the raindrops pattering high above me.

Friends and family who have been here almost always say, "This place sure has character!" That means, I think, that the cabin is unique, different, with little oddities and idiosyncrasies not found in a typical home. There are friends and relatives who say, partly because I choose to live in an old log cabin in the woods with nary another home in sight, "That guy is a real character." That, too, means unique, different, with oddities and idiosyncrasies that make me a bit strange. I'm not sure that use of "character" is complimentary, but it is often said with an affectionate smile or grin, and then I can certainly accept that description as my own.

There is, though, another use of the word "character". To me it means strength of purpose, the will to deal with the tough times that life can bring, undying faith and trust in others and in yourself. I've known many strong women throughout my life, women with just that sort of "character". My sister, who lived joyously as multiple sclerosis took a horrible toll on her body, comes particularly to mind.

That kind of character does not come easily to men, particularly younger men, I think. Too many distractions, most of them wearing skirts. (I grin as I write this, but I'm too old to recall *why* I grin). Although in times of war and emergencies of all kinds, young men may well find "character" pushing them to leap into the line of fire to save another's life. And many young men in the world of work will find "character" driving them to leave a job and leap into the unknown because that job of theirs was causing harm to others in some way. Still, I think that this sort of character is even more likely to be found in old men, men with fewer distractions, men nearing the end of their years who can use their remaining time to grow in understanding and in faith and trust, and even in love for others who make up humanity.

One day, perhaps, I will merit the comment from a friend or relative, "He has real character." That is the use of the word that is most important in this old cabin of mine and in this old world of ours. This is as close as I ever come to "preaching" on a Sunday morning. Just thinking, as my mind went off in a particular direction, amused at the different uses to be made of one world, as I had my cup of coffee this morning. Solitude can do that to you.

Falling In Love

Have you ever leaped from the high diving board at some community pool? You'll never forget the first time. I was visiting a college buddy who had graduated a year ahead of me, found a good teaching job in an Iowa town, and had married one of the most beautiful women I have ever seen. They told me to pack my bathing suit. It was a gorgeous summer day in Iowa, and the huge community pool looked oh, so inviting. Eager to impress the lovely lady he'd married, I climbed to the high board and ... Oh, man! That pool looked no bigger than a bathtub! I was scared silly, wondering what would happen if I didn't land just right, but I was up there, and I had to do it. I bounced around a little, then dove straight down, falling, falling, falling, and SPLASH! Made it!

I guess that's why they call it "falling" in love. It's like diving for the first time. One minute you're standing there, feet firmly planted on the ground, and then this person comes strolling past. Suddenly you find yourself on the high diving board. Oh, you may bounce around a little bit. Love can be pretty scary, you know. No idea how you'll land. Land wrong and there's a lot of pain. But then you throw caution to the winds and fall. You fall! That's the easy part, the falling. The hard part is figuring out whether you really want to do this, or not, before you fall. That, and the landing. It's got to be just right, or there's going to be pain. For somebody. Maybe you. But if all goes well, you trade your bathing trunks in for a tuxedo, or your little two-piece number in for a long white dress, and you've made it!

I've been falling in love for several weeks now. The young lady is in her late twenties, and very beautiful. I see her here at the cabin three or four nights a week. Oh, she's not the sharpest tack in the box, as they say, but she can hold her own in a conversation. She's a working girl, a server in a restaurant, and while she doesn't make a fortune at it, she does well enough to have her own place. I'm kind of proud of her, actually. I do worry a bit about how it will all end, and when, but at my age I'll take whatever time with her I can get. I guess that's love.

You may know her. Her name is Penny, and she's a star in "The Big Bang Theory" on television. I catch all the re-runs.

Beaumont R. Hagebak

Falling Out Of Love?

Looking back some seventy years or more, I don't believe I have ever fallen out of love. Or crept, crawled, walked, ran, or flew out of love. Sometimes I've tried, but I have never succeeded. I keep right on loving, willy-nilly, even if that wonderful "other" slams the door in my face. Maybe that's true of you, too?

I do build boxes though. Heart-shaped, soft-lined boxes that capture the loves that once were and hold them in a particular time, a particular place. I can come back to peer into one box or another, and revisit with a smile that time and that place and that person who once meant love to me. I'll admit, it sometimes takes me a while to build a box because pain and hurt limit my motivation. But eventually the box appears filled with its own time, its own place, and a person I still love in that particular time, in that particular place.

Sometimes boxes like those can be forgotten for a while. Eight years ago, a letter appeared in our mailbox addressed to me from a woman in Oregon whose name and return address weren't at all familiar to me. I was almost afraid to open it. Danger used to fall out of trees several generations ago. Today, danger more often falls out of envelopes. "If you aren't the Beaumont Hagebak who lived in Sisseton, South Dakota when you were in first grade, please just destroy this letter," the writer said. I was that little boy, so I continued to read. "We were in love with each other in first grade," the letter went on. "I remember holding your hand on the playground during recess, and having you push me on the swings." In my mind's eye, I found that box and peeked into it. There she was, my first-grade love, standing by the swings.

Her family left Sisseton before second grade began and returned a year later just as my family was moving to Minnesota. We never saw one another again. She became a poet and playwright, and I became a psychologist and professor. Sixty-seven years later, she found me on the internet and, on a dare from friends, wrote the letter to me. My wife and I were planning a trip to Washington state, and arranged to visit my first-grade love in Oregon and take her out to dinner. She and I still write to one another, primarily during the holiday season. I can open that box and peer into it anytime I want to revisit that special time and that special place that was first grade.

I truly believe that we may fall in love, but once that happens, special times and places are created that belong with the loved one. We don't "fall" out of love. If we don't let anger, hurt, or hate overwhelm us, we still love. We love the significant other in a place and time unique to that person. Here in this mountain cabin I can return to that unique person, and relive memories of a certain place, a certain time, and continue to love.

And I don't even have to leave my recliner...

Love And Marriage...

One of the problems with a solitary life in the north woods of Georgia, or anywhere else for that matter, is that you have time to think. Today I was thinking about love and marriage. I probably should have been doing a nice watercolor instead.

There's an old song written by Sammy Cahn and sung by Frank Sinatra that goes: "Love and marriage, love and marriage, go together like a horse and carriage..." I say "HORSEFEATHERS!"

Love and marriage go together like a *horseless* carriage. And what's a "horseless carriage" you may ask, if you're younger than I am? It's an automobile. That's what it is. And that's a piece of machinery that is almost impossible to put together. Everything's got to fit just right, or you wind up with a "lemon". And it's got to stay together for a long time, or you wind up with a "junker". And along the way it's bound to get some dents, and scratches, and maybe even wind up "totaled".

I've loved, in a spiritual sense, whole hosts of ladies, all of them beautiful. Just yesterday, for example, I fell madly in love with the young lady who was drawing my blood for testing. I was stark staring crazy about my high school girlfriend, as her father would have been the first to tell you. I married a little Quaker girl and had three sons with her. I married a girl of Austrian descent, too, after my Quaker girl walked away one day mumbling something about "lemons". My Austrian left after forty years. Those Austrians have stamina. Now, at age eighty-one, I have struck up conversations with ladies I have known for years and those I have known for days, and all with the same result. That is, no result at all. My horseless carriage is horribly dented. Maybe even totaled. . .

At this advanced age, living as I do in an old log cabin in the woods where few ladies would be willing to visit, much less stay the night, I have determined that putting together a new horseless carriage would be impossible. For one thing, I can't remember why it would be important that a lady stay the night. I do have two guest bedrooms though. I can cook pretty well, the cabin is always clean (one old guy doesn't dirty it up much), and I shower regularly. Sometimes I even shave. But I don't want "love and marriage", even if they go together. Love alone would suit me just fine. Maybe I should have kept that big old dog.

How Are Things . . . ?

Went to see my financial advisor down in Atlanta the other day. I drove. Don't *ever* do that! Hire a small plane and parachute in. Bumper to bumper, and half of it huge trucks. Get too close to one of those and you can't see the highway signs. Blocked by the trucks. But I got there and got back, and according to the expert, I'm doing just fine financially if I die tomorrow. Slept well last night. But somehow, the events of the day got me to thinking about the upper-Midwest where I grew up.

I wrote some songs…to be sung to the tune of "How Are Things in Glocca Morra".

Minnesota (It's spelled with a "t" but pronounced with a "d")

How are tings in Minnesoda?
Do dey still eat lutefisk up dere?
Do da blonde girls still look cute and nice,
But cold as ice,
And guys wear facial hair?

How are tings in Minnesoda?
Do da Vikings still play ball up dere?
Do da snowmobiles still rule da road,
After it's snowed?
(Cars can't drive anywhere.)
How are tings in Minnesoda?
Does ice hocky still draw crowds up dere?
Does da summer still last just one day?
Dat's what they say.
But I'm not sure dat's fair.

WISCONSIN (Some people pronounce it "Visconsin." Dose would be my people.)

How are tings in old Visconsin?
Do da Germans still brew beer up dere?
Do da Cheeseheads still make cheese all day,

And curds and whey?
Do girls still braid their hair?

Enough, already!

Maybe, living alone in this old log cabin with a cat gives me a little too much time to think. Or not to think. You're the best judge of that. Have a glorious day.

Mad As A Wet Hen!

When my mom talked about angry people or was even angry herself (an unusual state of being for that sainted lady), she would say they, or her, were "as mad as a wet hen." I can't imagine that she ever sprayed water on a hen, but then I can't imagine my conception either. Can you imagine yours? I doubt it. Anyhow, I grew up with the phrase "as mad as a wet hen".

Today, for some reason or for no reason at all, I am "mad as a wet hen". I've tried to pin it down. There's the loss of family and friends. I should take down that picture I have on the file near this computer that was made of the Blue Earth High School Class of 1954 during our fiftieth reunion. Many of those well-known and well-loved faces are gone now. Makes me mad. There's living with squirrels, too. They really "tick me off". There's that stack of stuff that needs to be filed but hasn't been filed because I just don't like filing, and that makes me mad. It's hotter than it has any right to be outside today, "hotter than a piss ant eating a bale of hay". For those of you unfamiliar with that terminology, a "piss ant" is a very tiny reddish ant that tends to congregate in unpleasant areas where there aren't indoor toilets, and couldn't eat a bale of hay if its life depended on it. I'm angry at the State of California, which is trying to hold me responsible for an abandoned car I once owned but sold a year ago to CarMax. Georgia would treat me better. I'm not happy with the politics of the day. Many aren't. But I'm just mad as a wet hen.

Sure, I have a great deal to be thankful for. And the value of those people, and those things, that I am thankful for far outweighs this temporary lapse in sanity. I have a wonderful family, many don't. I have a log home that is safe for me to sleep in at night, and many don't have a home at all. I have grand dreams that lead me to write in the hope of publishing, and to paint in the hope of astounding people with the beauty of what I may be able to do. Many have no dreams. I have friends that I care for as they care for me, and I am grateful and deeply touched by those friendships. Many have few friends. I have health at age 81 that allows me to do my own cooking, and cleaning, and bathing, and dressing, and all the ADL's ("activities of daily living") that many my age simply can no longer do. And I can still work within my community to make life better for so many, if I try.

I think, on re-reading this piece, it's high time I quit being "mad as a wet hen" and begin to work harder than ever before to make my world a better place for all creatures, people included. Particularly the people I love. I'm through with that anger that led me to begin this piece. No purpose served by it. The greater purpose in life, yours and mine, is to make this old world of ours a better place than the one we came into years ago. And don't let anybody spray water on you for whatever you can do to achieve that goal. OK?

Sorry. Guess I became the "preacher" that my grandma always wanted me to be. This is as close as I come to that, grandma

Thoughts On A Sad Day

The power went out in our mountain neighborhood at about 4:00 this morning, and finally came back on just before 6:00. Sometime early this morning our friend, Dee, died. Cancer, diagnosed only a few short weeks ago. The time was way too brief, and the loss way too great. She was a quiet person, friendly though, and caring. I got to know her because we often sat near one another at social events, just luck of the draw. Her husband, Warren, had become a good friend — the man who always seemed to make sure that I was invited to, or at least knew about, activities and events here in Lake Arrowhead. He sort of watched out for me, you might say.

It's hard to know what's really needed on days like this one. I wrote Warren a brief letter, telling him that this old cabin was always open to him, and that he was welcome anytime he wanted to talk with a friend, or just sit with one. I don't want to interfere in this trying time, but I did want him to be sure to know that I would be available for him. It's not easy thing to lose a loved one. Often, just knowing that others care can ease the pain and lighten the load of grief. At least, that's how it seems to me. That's been my experience, and probably yours, too.

I'm reading a book just now by a British writer, P. D. James. Normally I find the writings of English authors to be a bit dull, the stuff to fall asleep by in an overstuffed chair with a glass of red wine on the nearby table. P. D. James is not cut from that cloth. At one point in this book, she describes a man who realizes that he has lived his whole life with the expectation of it ending. It was, he says, "never a serious worry, but the thought was always there." I doubt that's true for the young, but for many of us in our "senior years" thoughts of death are never far away. Our friend, Dee, was young by the standards I set now at age 81, and so probably didn't concern herself about her own death until the cancer came. Caring for others was far more her style.

And so, today is a sad day for those of us who live on Corner Oak Court, and for the many others who are just learning that Dee is gone. The thoughts and prayers of many will be with Dee and Warren today and in the days to come. We are few, we who live in this mountain neighborhood, and we all want to offer some sort of tribute to our friend. This is just about the only way I know of to offer mine.

Four Musings On A Friday Afternoon

Friday afternoons, even for older retirees, are times for taking stock, for thinking back in time, for making future plans, and for just marveling at life's moments. This was such a Friday. A whole bucket list of things to get done, and every one of them can wait until tomorrow.

Routines change when you add two legged, four legged, or (deliver us!) eight legged creatures to your household. The big black cat with four white paws has been a cabin dweller now for a couple of weeks. I used to have coffee in my recliner, then head for the computer to begin the day. Now, when I head for the computer, so does she. If I'm fast enough, I can get the screen up and running before she joins me. Usually I'm not fast enough. She walks across the computer table, tail in the air, purring loudly, and expecting to be petted and spoken to for at least half an hour. It's not possible to see the screen (small screen, large cat) so she does get petted and spoken to. I'm running half an hour late at the dawn of each morning now. My routine is shot. Pleasantly.

My sons stay in touch. Today it was my eldest, Beaumont William, checking in with an aggravating tale indeed. He's moving to Athens, Georgia from Texas, and all his furniture was loaded onto an American Van Lines truck that was to have arrived in Athens in two days. He did. So did his mother, who will be living with him. It's now been a week without furniture, sleeping in sleeping bags and on those blow-up mattresses donated to the cause by friends who also donated a couple of camping chairs. The story about a railroad strike causing the delay sounded a little "fishy", but what's a guy to do? Some of his money will be refunded on Sunday, when the truck is now to arrive. I invited them to stay here for a couple of days, but he has a large dog and I have a large cat, and never the twain shall meet. "But," he says, "the water works anyhow." Always find the bright side, if at all possible.

A couple of my trees will have to go. These are two sixty-foot tall oaks, joined at the base, and deader than doornails. (Where did that phrase come from, anyhow?) I tried to talk the tree removal expert into the notion that they were just one tree, cutting my costs in half, but that attempt failed miserably. I got the written permissions from the Homeowner's Association, which was easy, considering the fact that the trees really were deader than doornails. So, a call came in last night from the expert saying, "You know that we'll be out tomorrow morning, because somebody called you, right?" "No, nobody called me." "Oh, gosh! There must be some kind of mixup. I'll check it out and call you back." So far, no call back but no tree cutters either. Maybe it was a railroad strike?

The lady at the Post Office spoke to me this morning. "What do you think about what's going on in this country?" How do you answer that in a Post Office line? "I don't think the President knows, either." That's what I said. Got a sad nod back. Whew! Politics can drive you crazy!

Sunday Afternoon Musings

Another Sunday. A quiet day with plenty of time to think. This Sunday I'm thinking about those intrepid souls who came before me. What triggered this sort of musing? I have no idea. But here I am, back in the 1800's and moving to America with people who are my people.

The people on the Hagebak side of the family were farmers, struggling to make it on a small rocky bit of ground known as "Hagabakken" just outside of Selbu, Norway. John Haldorson and his wife, Beret Olsdatter Svinaas had ten children. Farm children in Norway at that time were often sent off to find their own way in the world at age twelve. Life was hard. Their son Ole herded cattle in the mountains at that tender age, and later was a commercial fisherman in the Lofoten Islands farther north. He married, and very likely then pushed for the family to move to Minnesota, where land was free to settlers willing to farm it. A new life in a new land held promise.

Ten members of the family left Selbu in 1867—the grandparents John and Beret, Ole and Ingeborg and their infant daughter, and five other children and young adults—boarding the "Neptunus" in Trondheim for a seven-week sailing to Quebec. From there, they traveled to Minneapolis, arriving on July 4, "Independence Day". Three years were spent in nearby Brooklyn Center while the family worked to get a team of oxen and supplies for homesteading. They then made the trek across Minnesota to Lac qui Parle County on the far western border, built homes of sod, and began to farm the land. Grasshoppers swarmed their land in 1873 and again in 1877. During those two years, Ole was able to gather only twenty bushels of wheat—their entire crop. Somehow, life went on.

Beret was lonesome for her home, "Hagabakken", in Norway. She persuaded all of the family members except her husband, John, to take the name "Hagebak" as a way of remembering the home that harsh economic reality had forced them, and almost a third of Norway's population at that time, to leave. Today, there are only a couple of dozen "Hagebaks" by name, but over 600 people with direct links to Beret and John and their children.

And so I sit here in my log cabin in North Georgia this Sunday afternoon and marvel at the kind of people these ancestors must have been, who left the home they loved, the land they farmed, the nation they revered, to travel great distances under what can only have been harsh conditions, to reach a new world and begin a new life. Sturdy stock, proud people, who worked hard and achieved success. Amazing, when you think about it. How strange it must have felt to them, how many demands the journey made on them, how strong in spirit they must have been, how very brave. I so admire them.

Your ancestors were probably very much like them —sturdy, proud, hardworking, strong in spirit.

And I have stood on the land in Norway known as "Hagabakken", and I cried.

Just Thinking About Dumb Stuff

It's Sunday afternoon and there's a shimmering bright blue metallic party balloon stuck up high in one of the old oaks across the road. It could be something other than a party balloon, like maybe an "IT'S A BOY!" balloon, or even an "OPEN HOUSE TODAY!" balloon. There are one or two homes for sale in the neighborhood. It's less likely that it's an "IT'S A BOY!" balloon from somewhere on Corner Oak Court than a "IT'S A BOY GRANDCHILD!" balloon. Anyhow, it's up in a tree, way too high to climb up to, and it's driving me over the edge. (I was close to the edge anyway, as most of my neighbors down the road know.) ☺ I can see it clearly from my recliner.

At first, I thought the balloon was a patch of blue sky in an otherwise dreary, dark, cloudy, rainy old day. But it was just too bright. Maybe it was sent as a message from some deity or another to tell me not to worry about the hurricane winds and torrential rains coming later this afternoon. At this precise moment in time, the sixty-foot tall trees aren't moving much, and the rain has let up enough to allow me to take the trash out, but a few minutes ago those oaks and pines looked like drunken hula dancers. The storm is supposed to come right through Lake Arrowhead between 3:00 and 9:00 p.m. today. Not much to fear up here, though. It would take quite a wind to pick this old log cabin up and move it around much. As for flooding, the cabin is on the high ground.

My neighbors down below know that they can come up here if things get too damp down there. Not likely though. We all live on the side of a mountain. Water runs downhill. I do feel sorry for the very wealthy down by the lakeside, though. (Smile)

Wonder what happens to all the other bright and shiny metallic party balloons after the party's over. Or old used up kites, for that matter. Or those little balsa wood airplanes with a bit of lead in the front? Or all those tricycles we used to pedal around on when we were kids. Where the heck are they? And bicycles with fat tires? There aren't enough museums in all the world to hold all that stuff. Who, if anyone, is wearing all those old "leisure suits" so popular (until the moment I bought mine) in the 1960's? And what about facial hair shaved off men, or leg hair shaved off lovely ladies? (Oh, I know ladies use a different process now, but I am a single man and don't have a clue what that process might be). Where is all that hair? Ever been to a barber shop? Hair all over the floor. Where does it all wind up?

You may have noticed that I don't write about politics or religion (well, except for the old Norse gods, of course). I'm just too busy, trying to figure out all kinds of other stuff. Besides, I've never been able to figure out politics or religion, making me just like a whole lot of other folks I think. I'd prefer to deal with the easier stuff, like bright and shiny metallic party balloons caught in trees. Somebody has to do that, too, you know.

Well, it's getting on toward 3:00 in the afternoon, and the big winds are supposed to hit us soon. There's an open house at a home for sale down the road, and I'm looking forward to a pretty colorful, flying metallic balloon-filled time coming right up. Should be pretty exciting. I may even let the cat watch.

Doin' Nothin' Much

This morning I slept in, if you can call getting out of bed at 7:30 in the morning "sleeping in". Got the daily cup of coffee and fed the cat, then hit the recliner to watch the world come alive again. There were birds out there before the winter sun hit the tops of my tall trees, and a squirrel came by to see if he could grab some seeds before I could run him off. He couldn't, and I did run him off. The list of tasks for today was sitting beside the lamp, right where I'd left it. (I was kind of hoping it had disappeared during the night. No such luck.)

Today I was supposed to:

- Take stuff to the cleaners, like shirts, pants, tablecloth, and such;
- Get more suet blocks to insert into the hanging log that holds suet for the birds;
- Pick up more deer corn, and Mexican flavorings for making stuffed green peppers;
- Call the Ford dealer to get an appointment for the car's normal servicing;
- Call the tire people to get four new tires for the car;
- Pull together documents required to figure my taxes for 2017 — a strange year;
- Take out the trash and tidy up around here.

Well, here it is, early afternoon, and I'm still watching the birds. Haven't even picked up the mail. Mostly junk anyhow, with a few bills thrown in to make life exciting. The squirrel hasn't come back. I can be pretty scary when I want to be. I did look up the word "lethargy", but it doesn't seem to apply to me. I'm not having any serious physical or mental problems, which are required if you want to consider yourself lethargic. So, since I already had the dictionary in my lap, I looked up "lazy".

Ah, much better! "Resistant to work or exertion; disposed to idleness; slothful. To spend (time) in loafing." That's me today. "Slothful".

My shirts and stuff will get just as clean next Monday. We're in a warming trend (finally) so the birds don't *need* suet. I have a couple of days' worth of deer corn rolling around in the trunk of my car and I need to clean that up anyhow. I've got a very nice green pepper, ground beef, and an onion—I might just invent a Norwegian style Mexican dinner. (No spices, just salt and pepper. Norwegian spice racks are quite small). I wouldn't be able to get the car in for servicing and tires until next week even if I called today. Taxes aren't due until mid-April. The cabin looks pretty good, since there's only me to mess it up. And if I wait long enough, the trash may take itself out. No worries.

I don't believe in a whole lot of stuff. I do believe, though, that from time to time a man should just pour himself a glass of cabernet sauvignon, grab a good book as he passes by the bookcases, plunk himself down in the recliner, and just lean back. I do believe in Norwegian Lutheran guilt, of course, having been raised with it as a constant companion throughout my childhood. But I've been working for sixty or more of my eighty-one years to beat that back, with enough success to allow me this one day to wallow around in "slothfulness". My cat is a good role model for this wallowing around. She's been "slothful" all day today…and every day, come to think of it. But of course, she doesn't have stuff to take to the cleaners.

5. Companions Of The Furry Kind

Friends with built-in fur coats are standard issue for people living in these Appalachian Mountains. I had to leave my dear cat behind in California, and soon my ex-wife let me know that she had been "put to sleep". So, after a time, I began to think about getting a kitten. Then I did get a dog that just didn't fit my lifestyle. Finally, I got a large ten-year-old female cat named "Putih". These are stories about those friends.

One Last Tear For Little "Bella"

When California dropped behind me in the rearview mirror, I had many regrets. One of the big ones was that I had to leave our old gray cat, "Bella", behind. She'd been a member of our household for seventeen years, and I knew I'd miss her. But "Bella" loved our California home, with its fenced back yard, a small pond for mosquito fish, evergreen shrubs and trees and rocks to hide behind. There was a patio with a roof, and chairs with soft, comfortable cushions. At night, she slept at the foot of our bed. By day she'd usually find a lap to sit in if she wasn't out in the back yard. "Bella" was a small ball of love, and we loved her right back.

My wife (the divorce is not final until early August) contacted me by e-mail yesterday to tell me that she'd had to have "Bella" put down. Too much chronic pain and a host of internal ailments had made our little gray cat's life miserable. She'd hide under our bed, and she'd cry in pain whenever she was up and around. I told my wife in an e-mailed response that I certainly agreed with her decision, based on the description she gave me of our cat's pain. Of course, I did. We have dealt with just such necessities before. You probably have, too. It's in the nature of the relationships we have with our pets. And then I found time to cry.

I'm not much of a believer in things I can't see, touch, smell, or taste. And this old log cabin is a long way from California—almost as far away as a person can get in the continental United States. Distance divided us, that loving little gray cat and me, but I'm in tears as I write this, so saddened by the loss of a little friend who used to sit in my lap and purr. Distance divides me from so many lives that I cherish, and I care deeply about each of them. Tonight, I'm shedding one last tear for our "Bella", and I'm not ashamed to admit it.

Thoughts On (Maybe) Getting A Kitten

Cherokee County, Georgia, has an outstanding pet adoption and care facility—a beautiful new building not far from town. Pictures of available pets, including rabbits and birds, are on the Internet. The dogs and cats they adopt out to families have all their shots and are neutered. For only $100, a family can adopt a new family member...*if* the family passes muster. You have to be the right match. Some animals prefer homes with other pets, or with noisy children, and some do not. The family has to fit in, just as much as the pet does. I kind of like that notion.

I've wanted a pet to be with me here at the log cabin ever since I realized that 22-year-old college educated young women willing to live in the woods with an 81-year-old guy were in short supply. Tried a large dog for a week, but the deer I feed weren't any too happy about that. And I have had a few problems with mice, now pretty much taken care of, but a cat would be an ally in dealing with that problem. So, probably a kitten? Well, there *are* things to consider:

- A kitten would probably outlive me, and what then? Maybe I should consider an ancient cat instead, to more likely match my own life expectancy—and my rather sedentary lifestyle. Do old cats drink red wine, I wonder?

- I'd have to have an indoor cat. While life outdoors in the city can be hazardous at best, this crazy place has *bears*!!

- It should probably be a female cat. Female cats are just easier to get along with, I think. Having raised three sons, I actually know that for a fact.

- My friends and neighbors up here in the woods all seem to have dogs, in some cases *multiple dogs*. Am I a good enough psychologist to help a kitten understand that those big, lumbering, noisy, barking, sniffing creatures can be your friends? I doubt it. I'm not totally convinced, myself.

- Some of my relatives are allergic to cats. They walk into the house, sniff cat dander, and run right back out again. We'd have to sit out on the patio. It can get pretty cold out on that patio in February.

- An indoor cat could perch up on the top of the sofa (I used to call it a "davenport" but got laughed at so often that it became a sofa) and look outside through the glass living room wall. There are hummers, birds, deer, squirrels, chipmunks, bears, raccoons, big scary insects, and stuff out there that could give a cat sensory overload. The last thing I need around here is a crazy cat suffering from way too much visual stimulation.

So, I'm still thinking. The county pet adoption facility opened at 10:00 this morning, but I have workmen coming at 11:00. Maybe that's the deity's way of telling me to back off and think it all through very carefully. But I may just stop out there this afternoon, just to look around, you understand. Can't hurt, right?

A Dog's Tale

This is a story about a wonderful eleven-year-old Doberman mix, female, strong and fearless, who became part of my life up in this log cabin for a short while. In the six days she was with me, she taught me many things about dogs, homes in the forest, and myself.

My sons and their families all have dogs—at least one. They enjoy the companionship of dogs. And dogs do make great companions. Since I was alone in a cabin in the North Georgia woods, it seemed obvious that I needed a companion. This dog needed a companion, too. Her human parents both were elderly and died, the last one a month ago. I had been trying to keep dog ownership at bay, but when I heard about the needs of this old girl—her name is "Maxine"—even I said, "Yes, I'll take her." Nobody in the family had really seen her, and we all thought she was a small black lap dog. Wrong! This lady weighed in at close to seventy pounds. One of my sons picked her up after work one evening, bought her a new bed, pink collar, bowls, treats—the works. Realizing that she hadn't been bathed in a long time, he even took her to a groomer who worked late to make that dog sparkle. My son was surprised at her size, but still wanted to help her and his dad, and so he brought her up to North Georgia that very night.

This old cabin is a smallish sort of place, and her bed alone took up about a third of my living room. There's just one entrance that has no steps up and down, and it wasn't the entrance with the built-in doggie door. Maxine would not climb stairs. I found that she would eat only the treats we had for her—none of that dog food, please. And she, a city girl who had never seen a deer before, took an instant dislike to those deer who were frequent visitors to my home. I guess she liked squirrels because she never went after them (more the pity), but she'd almost rip my leash-toting arm off wanting to chase those deer.

The last day she lived here as my companion, I realized that the hummingbird feeder was empty, brought it in, and filled it with sugar water. Maxine hadn't been out to pee for several hours, and drank copious amounts of water, so I figured we'd kill two birds with one stone (so to speak) and take her out with me to replace that feeder. I checked first for deer. None around. Out we went. And would you believe that it was at that precise moment that three deer decided to stroll by?

Good old Maxine, intent on protecting me from those fearsome creatures, charged off in hot pursuit! Still holding the leash, I was slammed into an old oak tree, lost my grip on the leash, and dropped the full container of hummingbird food. Down I went, my artificial hip slamming into the wet ground! I screamed in pain. Wonder of wonders, Maxine gave up the chase and came running back to see if she could help me. Amazing. I got to my knees—one of them is artificial, too—and pulled myself upright. There was still a bit of hummer food in the feeder, so Maxine and I hung up the container and headed for the cabin.

My son picked Maxine up that very night. She had a new home with a nice family within one day.

I'm learning to walk again. All's well that ends well.

The Cat Saga, Part One

August 8, 2017, The Day I Got The Cat!

7:30 a.m. Rise and shine. Shower, shave, put on a clean shirt, head downstairs.

8:00 a.m. Brew my coffee in the Keurig thing, take hummer feeder back outside, drink coffee while looking at the rainy world and worry about becoming a cat "owner" again. (You don't "own" the cat, the cat owns you.)

9:00 a.m. Former caretaker arrives with food, treats, scratching posts, and dishes. This is a wealthy cat I'm getting! We talk "cat" stuff. I continue worrying.

9:15 a.m. Make breakfast—one egg, two slices of bacon, a nectarine, orange juice, and about 20 pills in varying shapes and sizes. I eat and worry.

9:45 a.m. Dishes in the dishwasher, hand wash the frying pan, make up grocery list for tomorrow. The caretaker can return now with the cat's toilet and the cat, anytime. I worry.

10:00 a.m. Phone call from former caretaker. "I'll be there in about an hour." "Well, don't forget the cat toilet." "I won't!" "And if the doors are locked and the lights are out, that means I've changed my mind." "You're joking, right?" "Yes." I have another hour to worry. Good. Wouldn't want to rush this.

11:15 a.m. The cat arrives in a cloth carrier, carried into the cabin by her former caretaker. The carrier is opened, the cat comes out, takes one look at me, and heads for a dark corner of the living room. Later, we searched that corner and then the cabin, but the cat was nowhere to be found. All doors and windows were shut, so she must be here. A magical disappearing cat. Doesn't know where her bathroom is. Worry, worry, worry.

12:00 p.m. The former caretaker leaves, and I am all alone with the cat—or not with the cat, depending on how you look at it. Kind of weird. We shall see. Worry.

The cat that now owns me is a 13-pound female, black and white with white paws, short haired.

She was born in Seattle, Washington, on September 1, 2007, making her almost ten years old. She has always been an indoor cat. Her name is "Putih Mittens" (pronounced "Pootee"), which is Indonesian for White Paws. She spent some time with a family that lived in Indonesia for a while. She'll figure this all out, once she dares to look around a bit.

So now I am no longer living alone. How's that for a major life change? I've got to go out and buy some cat toys—maybe tomorrow.

The Cat Saga: Part Two

Hey! We found the cat!

The former caretaker of the cat, who is now a guest in my cabin, brought her here around noon on Tuesday. She was not terribly happy to have to leave the cat carrier they brought her in, and she crept along the living room floor, belly dragging on the carpet, to hide behind my two-drawer lateral file. We caretaker types chatted a while, and when we went to check on the cat, she was no longer there! The magical disappearing cat had disappeared. From noon on Tuesday to well past my bedtime on Thursday night, I had not seen hide nor hair of that cat.

My son, "Hawk", found her at suppertime Thursday, hiding under a small two-drawer cabinet I use as an end table beside the sofa, but she wouldn't come out. And I can't bend over far enough to be able to say that I saw her. For almost 60 hours she hid out, not eating, not drinking, not using her own litter box. Before going to bed, I left a few treats and her water dish near the place she had been seen by Haakon.

This morning, lo and behold, she had a few sips of her water, found her food dish in the kitchen, and had eaten a late evening meal, and had even used her litter box in the laundry room. She must have done a bit of exploring in the night. The way my cabin was built, the doors to all three bedrooms and the two bathrooms can be shut and were. The rest of the cabin—downstairs and upstairs and on the stairs and under the stairs—is wide open. But my kitty cat is no longer under the cabinet, though. I've gone around with a flashlight and have yet to find her hiding place. We are making progress, though. At this rate, she will be sitting on my lap sometime in 2021 A.D. So, I haven't sent any pictures of her to everyone yet.

HOWEVER, on a positive note, the chipmunk has found a lady friend, or the lady chipmunk has found a guy. They move too fast for me to check on which is which. So, they race around out there like a couple of kids—just like you once probably did.

HOWEVER, tonight the mother deer showed up in my yard to show off her beautiful child, still spotted like "Bambi". I asked them to wait, and went and got them some corn, in violation of Lake Arrowhead rules and all that is holy, I guess. See, they are in between springtime berries and late summer acorns, and I'm a pretty soft touch. But the ears on the fawn are so very thin that you can almost see through them, and the legs are nothing more than matchsticks. What's a guy to do?

The Cat Saga: Part Three

Today is August 13, a full five days since I got this magical disappearing cat that I live with.

Today is the day that "Putih" (pronounced "Pootee" I think, at least that's how I pronounce her name) walked over to me and sniffed my hand. Twice. Then she wandered all over the main floor of the cabin, checking everything out. Apparently both the cabin and I passed inspection. Cats are pretty fussy, so I feel truly honored. Perhaps she finally realized that I am her best hope for cat food, water, treats, and a clean litter box.

"Putih" is a beautiful black and white adult indoor cat, with white paws, ten years old on September 1. Now she and I are going to be buddies, I do believe. A few more days and she'll probably want me to pat her head. She's not receiving visitors as of yet, but that's not too far off. She's more than a little bit shy.

Today I have a social event to attend down in Marietta, but when I get back up this way I plan to shop for a fine new litter box with a top for privacy and buy her several toys, too. Ladies seem to love toys. I think of jewelry as toys for human ladies. Cats seem to prefer toys that move. I'll also get some air freshener, I think. It couldn't hurt.

The Cat Saga: Part Four

The new cat, ten-year-old "Putih", has now been a resident of this log cabin for eleven days.

For the first three days, she was impossible to find, even though this is a smallish sort of cozy place. She's black, with a little white trim and pure white paws—enough white to make her truly interesting—and since this place is made of logs there are deeply dark "hidey holes" where a black cat, even one with white paws, can blend into the woodwork. When she finally did come out, it was with fear and trembling, but a girl has to eat after all, and use the toilet occasionally. So, these first forays into the light of day were short and to the point: "Where's my food dish?"

That lasted less than a week, though. The other day she decided to check out this old man who seems to talk to himself. Actually, I used to talk to myself—and quite intelligent conversations were held, I must say in all modesty. But when the cat arrived, I talked to her. Couldn't see her, so it was pretty much the same thing, but done in cat talk: "Hey, Putih, how are you this morning? Doing fine? I see you had your dinner after I went to bed last night. So, what's your plan for the day?" Actually, her plan for the day is to sleep. She's the most nocturnal critter I've ever lived with, and you may recall that I raised boys. Talk about nocturnal!

Well, yesterday when I sat down in my recliner to have my coffee, Putih came waltzing out from inside the piece of furniture that holds my television set, lay down on the floor in front of me, rolled around, purred loudly, and then demanded that I scratch her head, ears, and back. I guess we were friends then. When my coffee was gone, I moved over to my computer to see all the brilliant things that had happened in Facebook while I'd been sleeping—most of it having to do, one way or another, with Donald Trump. Uffda. Not terribly brilliant, either. Just as I was about to add my two cents worth (an ancient phrase taught to me by my mother), this cat leaps up in front of the screen, strolls back and forth, tail in the air, again in need of head scratching. Smart cat. Kept me from seeing Facebook stuff and blocked me from commenting. She stepped onto my keyboard, apparently wanting to make a comment herself, but soon got bored with that and strolled off. (To be fair, it took me quite a while to learn to use the computer, too.)

She went through the same routine this morning. I think she likes me. But then, what's not to like? (Don't ask my two ex-wives. They'll tell you! ☺ It will take hours and bore you to tears).

Putih is asleep now. It's daytime. There are birds all over the bird feeder, three hummers are fighting one another over by the hummingbird feeder (do they ever get to drink the sugar water?), the deer will come by soon looking for a handout, and the squirrels keep watching to see if any seeds drop from the bird feeder. Putih should be up and about. She's missing out on all the fun. But then, who knows what she does in the middle of the night?

The Cat Saga: Part Five

This was an awesome day in the world of cats! "Putih" climbed the stairs in the cabin, all the way to my second-floor sanctuary—my little art studio, my private bathroom, my walk-in closet, and the large bedroom where I can listen to rain on the roof. She had never dared do that before.

It's Monday, October 9, 2017—Leif Erikson Day! The day we celebrate the Viking discoveries of North America. While many people celebrate that "Johnny-come-lately" Italian, Christopher Columbus, those of us in the know celebrate the Vikings who landed their longships here a full 492 years before Columbus crossed the ocean blue. He didn't even get to the mainland, but just piddled around some offshore islands. But I digress. This was about my cat.

So, my cat decided to celebrate Leif Erikson Day by climbing the thirteen open stairs to the second floor of the cabin. As usual, I got up, shut the door from the bedroom to the studio so as not to scare people who might drive by and look up at the lights to see me stark nekkid and preparing to shower. I turned on the lights, did my manly man chores (brush teeth, comb hair, deodorize underarms, shave, splash on some "Brut" aftershave), dressed, and opened the door. And there was Miss "Putih", my brave cat, racing down the steps as fast as her little legs would carry her. She'd made it all the way up, and all the way back down. An amazing feat of bravery!

"Putih" has made tremendous strides since she arrived at the cabin on August 8. She hid for the first three days—no food, no water, no toilet. Her first forays into the living room were tentative at best, but then one day when I was taking a short nap in my recliner, she leaped into my lap. "Yikes", I shouted! "Putih" yelled "Meow!" and leaped down, clawing my pants leg to shreds. But now she considers my rather ample lap to be her territory, and purrs with contentment as she kneads my chest and stomach. (I'm black and blue from my waist to my neck). If you visit us, she is just likely to come over, sniff your shoe, and if that passes muster, she will climb into your lap. "Any friend of my dad's is a friend of mine," she seems to think.

Until today, "Putih" has often climbed into my lap, facing my dining area and the stairs, and stands there staring upstairs. She has huge eyes, and I will admit that it's pretty scary when she does that. Does she see something I don't? Ghosts, perhaps? I've come to believe, though, that she was just wondering what the heck is up there. Well, now she knows. So...I am very hopeful that those scary stares up the stairs (notice how cleverly I did that?) are a thing of the past. This old place with its bangs, and whangs, and creaks is scary enough without my cat seeing things that aren't there. (Or that I *hope* aren't there!)

So, today I have a brave cat. Impressive. I am so proud that I wanted to get it all down on paper. Hope you have a great and awesomely brave day yourself, dear reader.

Living With This Cat!

I'm really a pretty good psychologist—or was. Been retired for a long, long time now. But I've been a student (formal and informal) of human behavior most of my adult life. I even taught classes in human behavior, growth, and development in a couple of universities. Cat behavior? That's a whole 'nother thing again. I really don't think anybody understands cat behavior at all.

This cat I live with is a case in point. She sleeps downstairs. I sleep upstairs. When she hears me moving around up there at about 7:15 a.m., she heads over to the bottom of the stairs and waits. When I appear at the top of those stairs, she dashes away as fast as those four furry legs will carry her. That's probably a learned behavior. Once a week, it could be Friday, or Saturday, or even Sunday, is wash day. I put my dirty clothes and towels in a big laundry bag and—rather than risking life and limb by carrying the laundry down the stairs I simply drop it from on high. It makes a satisfying "WHAM" when it hits the floor. It's never hit the cat. She's not there. I must admit that I sometimes wonder what kind of sound it would make if it did hit the cat, but her instinct for self-preservation makes that pretty much impossible.

When I get downstairs, I make my daily cup of coffee and fill her bowls with cat food and water. As I trudge over to my recliner, this cat makes a bee-line for my chair. Once, I almost sat on her. So again, her instinct for self-preservation now keeps her from leaping into the recliner until I have settled my massive bulk into it first. She's pretty good at this self-preservation stuff. When she's finally in my lap, she will manage her position in order to place her right ear just over my heart. Perhaps she likes the sound—"blub, blub, blub". Or perhaps she was a cardiologist in an earlier life. Who knows? She doesn't say. I try to make no sudden moves. The other morning, I did move my left hand too quickly for her, and she dug her claws into it. Perhaps she was a surgeon in an earlier life? I've still got the scar.

On top of the old antique desk a few feet away, two model cars are displayed. One is a model of the first car I ever bought, a 1930 Ford coupe convertible with a rumble seat, for $25.00 when I was fourteen. The other is a model of the 1940 Ford coupe with a trunk that could hold a small army of classmates, the car I drove in high school when I was sixteen and seventeen and in love. This cat WANTS those two model cars—wants them badly. It could be the shiny chrome wheels that attract her. Or, possibly, she was a teenage boy in an earlier life. She'll never tell.

Lately she has been following me into the bathroom, where she waits for me to turn on the faucet in the sink. Then she wets her left paw and licks off the water before wetting it again. If I try to wash my hands when she's doing her wet and lick trick, she'll GROWL at me. Yes, GROWL!

I'm a bit of a prude when it comes to sharing a bathroom, but if I shut her out she'll sit outside the door and holler. "MEOW, DAMMIT!" At times like that, I'm glad that my closest neighbors are too far away to hear all that hollering. Sometimes I think she may have been a urologist or proctologist in an earlier life. I try to remind her regularly that "curiosity killed the cat", but she looks up at me as if she doesn't understand a word I'm saying. She does, though. I'm sure.

Maybe I should have gotten a hamster instead.

Guess Who Won!

This tale is about my cat, Putih, so you dog lovers might want to study it a bit. Putih comes home today after almost three months visiting friends while I was recovering from hospitalization, rehab center food, and catching up on e-mails, tax issues, the checkbooks, and all the stuff that real life is made of these days. Putih's homecoming either means that I am feeling much stronger and am now able to care for her properly, or that I have truly "flipped out" (a professional term) and no longer have a clue about what I'm doing. After yesterday, I am inclined to bet on the latter.

Richard and I had it all arranged. We had a Wednesday afternoon appointment with the vet to have Putih's nails clipped, and to give her the annual rabies shot. He got her into her carrying case and loaded her into my car—not so much as a teeny "Meow" out of her. Richard drove. We arrived ahead of schedule and were shown to a very nice private room with a built-in examination table for the cat, with a shelf beneath it, and a bench for humans right next to that. A little anxious wiggling from inside the carrying case, nothing to worry about. We were all set.

Moments later, a rather forceful young lady with a non-stop patter arrived to inform us of all the other cat items and services we should be purchasing. We did our best to ignore her. Since I had been married twice before, that was easier for me to do than it was for Richard. She was soon joined by a second young lady who took the top right off the carrying case. Putih was *exposed to the world*. She didn't like that one bit. With a hearty "Yowl" she leaped down to the bench on which I was sitting and dug her way in behind me with just her rather sizeable rear showing.

The young ladies went for Putih's rear, and Putih went for that shelf under the examination table.

A towel was thrown over her, but Putih made short work of that. Then one of the young ladies brought over a large piece of carpeting and attempted to wrap the cat in it. No such luck. Claws out and howling, Putih drove both ladies away. By that time, she was more than a simple house cat. Putih was a mountain lion, a fierce mountain lion, and mad as all heck! Black fur standing up all over the place made her look twice her normal size.

The vet arrived next, took in the situation, and said, "This cat is entirely too agitated and anxious to have her nails clipped today." Putih the cat had won!

The cat that will return to my log cabin today was reinserted into her carrying case with her long, sharp nails intact, and without any shots. At the front desk, I was given a small bag with a sedative and some instructions in it, and a bill for $146.00. We were told to come back in a year. I haven't really checked out the bag yet. Hope there's not a cat-nail clipper in it.

I may try the sedative myself before "Putih" arrives back home today. Can't hurt, can it?

6. Daily Routines And Other Weird Stuff

Here are a few stories about daily living in these mountains—the simple routines of a life lived alone. The routines, though, can be made more exciting by trying to drive on these mountain roads; by trying to drive on the roads of a big city; by dealing with my new-fangled phone and apologizing for being unable to do a very good job of that; by grocery shopping for foods that sometimes don't appear on Southern grocery store shelves; and by managing and taking a mountain of pills. (I'm old).

Routines (Daily)

Whoever you are, I know a little something about you. You know the same thing about me, I guess. We both have routines. Right? Things we do pretty much the same way at the same time, daily, weekly, yearly. It doesn't take much of a psychologist to figure that out. If you're observant, you may even begin to see individual routines and learn the behavioral patterns of others. Warren, for example, just walked by out in the road. He does that around eleven o'clock each morning. There's a small low patch in the hill I live on, and from there he can see me at my computer through the glass front of my log home. We wave. A shared routine. Routines are not the "spice" of life, but they help us maintain our balance. Think "normal". We do what we do when we do it because it grounds us, makes life seem "normal". Not a bad thing at all. Particularly since living in a log cabin in an oak forest in the North Georgia mountains is anything but normal!!

Every morning I get up at around 6:00 a.m., and head for the bathroom. Lights on, I grab clean underwear (yes, I do!) from the drawer, put it on the sink counter, tee shirt on top, and set up my "supplies". The order is always the same: toothbrush, hair spray, deodorant, shaving cream, aftershave lotion. Shower, do my cleanup chores, dress, grab my cane, head downstairs (very carefully!). Make my cup of coffee, settle into my chair, and watch the forested world outside for half an hour. Then, check my e-mails, maybe even Facebook, before heading into the kitchen for breakfast. It's usually about 10:00 a.m. by then. Might make just a slice of toast, or maybe an egg, and if I'm feeling really adventurous, I throw three slices of bacon into the frying pan. Always fruit—blueberries, strawberries, raspberries. Eat, clean the kitchen, and head either for the computer to work on stories or to the art studio back upstairs to paint with watercolors. Around 1:00 p.m. I heat up a Boar's Head beef and pork hot dog—no trimmings, no bread, just the hot dog held in a paper towel because it's hot! Then I'll usually read for a couple of hours. More writing or more art, then around 5:00 p.m. I'm out there in the yard feeding the birds and creatures of the forest who visit me regularly. The local news at 6:00 p.m., national at 6:30 p.m., and then I make dinner. The kind of dinner depends on my mood and energy level. I may fry up a pork chop, microwave a Vidalia onion with butter and a beef bouillon cube, and boil some corn-on-the-cob. Or I may just heat up a frozen dinner. Dessert is fruit or a cup of Jell-O pudding with caramel. Mmmmmm. Clean the kitchen, then check the e-mail and Facebook, and retire to my chair to watch television if there's anything good on (mostly not), and read, with a couple of glasses of wine. Off to bed at 9:30 p.m. Fill the CPAP tank with distilled water, brush my teeth, and "hit the sack". My day will begin again in about nine and a half hours (I sleep like I did when I was a teenager, except that I go to bed much earlier).

Routines (Weekly And Beyond)

The weeks have their routines, too. Wednesdays are always "town days", because I get an old man's discount at the grocery store on Wednesdays. So that's also the day that I pick up supplies for my computer, get a fifty-pound bag of field corn for the deer, take the used shirts and pants to the cleaners, stop at the drugstore for my meds, and maybe go to the bank. Tuesdays are "wash days", when I run the washer and dryer to first do darks, then whites. Since I have to be home then anyway, I typically write checks and worry about money on Tuesdays, sitting at the dining room (well, dining area) table. Fridays are "clean and vacuum" this place days. After cleaning the bathtubs on my knees a couple of weeks ago I could hardly walk, so I have hired a cleaning lady to come in once a month. She'll even dust the tops of the fan blades in the living room!! I can dust stuff in the meantime. The place is clean, though, in case visitors come around on Friday night or Saturday.

In case this all sounds pretty dull to you, please remember that this is a story about "routines". There are more out-of-routine things going on around here than you can "shake a stick at" (one of my mother's favorite expressions, and I still don't get it entirely). Friends stop by, always a joy. One got a new puppy this week and came by a few moments ago to show her to me. My 17-year old motorcycling granddaughter swung into my driveway just last week, low on gas and wanting to avoid the rain that was coming, and we talked about everything under the sun for a couple of hours! Great fun! The son who lives closest stops at various intervals to do some work around here that I can no longer do, or just to have a beer and talk to "old dad". Always nice. There are parties in the neighborhood and in the larger Lake Arrowhead community, and I am usually invited to join in the fun—and I don't feel like a "third wheel". And some days I just say to myself, "The heck with it!" and go off to do something entirely different! But it is routines that stabilize our lives and often give it meaning. Non-routine times can be grand—think "holiday season", for example. But we need those routines to keep our balance in this crazy old world!! I'm building some new ones that fit me in this wonderful place.

Driving These Mountain Roads

When I was fifteen, I wanted to become a long-distance trucker when I grew up. Either that or a stock car racer. Probably scared my folks silly. It is to their great credit that they said nothing, and as a result I never became a long-distance trucker or a stock car racer. I did, though, learn the words to a song: "Drivin' a truck on a mountain road, got a hot rod rig and I'm flyin' low, my eyes are full of diesel smoke, these hair pin curves ain't no joke! Diesel smoke, dangerous curves." There's a lot more to it than that, but you get the picture. He "had a girl at the bottom of the grade, she's got hot coffee already made ..."

Several times a week I drive my Ford down to Canton, about twelve miles away. No hairpin curves, but there's plenty of diesel smoke from the gigantic trucks that pass by headed the other way. It's a mountain road, up, down, around, two lanes and almost totally a "NO PASSING" zone.

Speed limit, 55 miles an hour.

Early this morning I was heading into Canton to get some essentials like pens and paper (hey, I was a college *perfesser*, so pens and paper are still considered "essentials"). Got behind a string of cars moving along at twenty-five miles an hour. On the top of a rise I could see about twenty cars ahead of me, led by a white car that was also going to Canton. Estimated arrival: tomorrow! An old guy in one of those huge old slab-sided cars so popular in the 1950's pulled in behind me. Behind him, in just a minute, a large truck joined the parade. Man, we had a convoy.

And then, three cars ahead of me, some guy driving a little red car decided he's had enough of these twenty-five miles an hour crap, AND MADE A U-TURN RIGHT IN THE MIDDLE OF THE HIGHWAY! Ever notice that guys who drive little red cars tend to be crazier than pet raccoons? Well, the lady behind him slammed on her brakes, the guy ahead of me slammed on his, and just to be polite I slammed on mine, too. So did the old guy in the slab-sided car from the 1950's. The guy driving the large truck behind him, though, was doing heaven knows what, and looked up to see that our convoy was now parked on the highway. Squeeeeeeeeel!! Braking like a madman, the truck pulled off the road onto the narrowest patch of grass in Georgia. You could hear him yelling, "Whoa, dang ya! Whoa!!" I figure he was raised on a horse farm. He managed to miss everything except a mailbox!

We went on, then, the two cars ahead of me, me and my Ford, the guy in the slab-sided 1950's car, and the large truck. The guy in the red car had pulled over, facing the other way, and if looks could kill, he'd be a goner right there at the side of the road. We caught up with the lead car quickly—it was only going twenty-five miles an hour, y'know—and made the three remaining miles to Canton in about an hour or so.

On my way home, there was a guy in a pickup truck carrying office furniture — desk, chairs, bookcase, and I don't know what else, all piled up high and nothing tied down. I kept my distance, drove twenty-five miles an hour, and he finally turned off the highway! Give us a shout: "Hallelujah"! And that's what driving in these mountains is all about. Hallelujah!! Made it again!

Sunday Travelin'

If you're thinking of driving through Atlanta, Georgia to get to somewhere else, I strongly recommend traveling on Sunday morning. Those huge trucks that clog the road are all but gone, the religious folk are in church, and there's nothing much on the road except you and a few other heathens.

I had decided to visit my son and his wife last Sunday in LaGrange, about 70 miles or so southwest of Atlanta. I also had a real dinner date with a lovely lady in Newnan, on the way back home to the cabin. The last time I tried this drive to points beyond Atlanta, just getting through the big city took an hour. That made the trip to LaGrange a three-hour marathon, and a scary one at that. Most of the time I couldn't even read the road signs because there were gigantic trucks on each side of my little Ford, and you can't see over or through them. But Sunday I made the entire trip, including a stop for gas, in precisely two hours. Drove into the parking lot beside my son's art studio just behind another car carrying him and his sweet wife, Pepper.

We had a great time. Drove down to Pine Mountain and Callaway Gardens. Atop Pine Mountain there is a great old stone and wood building overlooking miles and miles of nothing but forest. We had lunch. I ordered the "Country Fried Steak" with country gravy and fried okra as a side. I finished the steak, about half of the okra, and two glasses (well, fruit jars to be perfectly accurate) of unsweet tea. Here in the South you have to ask specifically for unsweet tea, or you'll get tea so rich in sugar that diabetes is almost sure to follow. And then we drove all through my old "stompin' grounds"—several rural counties where I worked years ago—before returning to my son's studio to watch a colleague of his building a paper maché horse. We all talked of art and life and had a wonderful catching-up time before I had to leave.

I had a "hot date" for dinner up in Newnan, about an hour north. Well, to be perfectly honest, at my age one no longer has "hot dates", but it was a nice warm friendly date. The lady was my secretary forty-five years ago, and I have aged appreciably. She, somehow, has not. Originally from Louisiana, she still speaks with that lilting accent so delightful on the ear. I was to find her home (which I did thanks to GPS), spend a bit of time meeting her two daughters and their children, and then take this lovely lady to an Italian restaurant. But it was the last day of the county fair, and her daughters and their kids never did get back home until nightfall. So, the lady set out an array of snacks and we talked. Until you have lived alone in a cabin in the woods, you cannot realize what a joy it is to simply talk with a lady who is there, not imaginary, and not a cat. And to top it off, her huge Boston Bull terrier, "Buster", took a shine to me. We became best buddies, he and I. Or maybe he was after my cheese. Ya'think?

As the day worked its way toward evening, we both realized we had completely forgotten about the Italian dinner we were going to have. She made me a sandwich, which I could only eat half of (never plan two big meals on the same day, particularly if one of them is "Country Fried Steak" with all the trimmings) and then I left to travel in the bit of daylight remaining in the day. Night blindness, with cars coming at you, is not a good thing for an older driver like me. It had been a spectacular Sunday, in every way. And I have been invited back to both LaGrange and Newnan. Must have done something right. Home safe and sound in my cabin, reflecting on a fine Sunday.

My Apologies ... But This Crazy Phone Of Mine ...

"Back in the day"...don't you just love that phrase? "Back in the day" can really mean almost anything, and it doesn't date you because "the day" is different for most everyone. High school "back in the day" for me was pretty different from high school "back in the day" for my granddaughters—even for my sons.

Well, "back in the day" (meaning during the summers when I was in college) I worked for a local phone company that specialized in small towns in Minnesota and Iowa. We dug a lot of holes, set a lot of poles, and one summer I was responsible for taking the wooden phones out of people's homes and replacing them with those nice new black rotary dial phones. "Wooden phones??" Children whose "day" was just a few years ago can hardly believe that there were ever such things as wooden phones!!

Well today I carry around a cell phone. It's about four inches tall and two inches wide, black, with a bad scar on the face of it. Maybe you remember that it fell out of my pocket into the oven when I was cooking a roast? Melted the lens for the camera that I guess is inside my phone. But I never took pictures with the thing anyway. I'm eighty-one, and I believe that cameras should be cameras and phones should be phones. Alexander Graham Bell and I were contemporaries.

Another thing I don't believe is that I can text message on this phone. It has a 2, and then so small they can hardly be read, an a b c Then there is a 3, followed by an equally small d e f And so on, ad nauseum. I can just barely get my fingers to push the 2 and the 3, but this phone expects me to spell "cat" for example by going 2-2-c, 2-a, and 8-t. As often as I was the last kid standing in the fifth-grade spelling bees, I really don't have the time (translation: "patience") to fool with this. CVS Pharmacy and my Minnesota friend C___ V_____, get pretty upset with me, but it's my phone and not some sort of spelling thingy. And what's this C and V thing anyway?

Missed calls? I have no idea how to answer one. If those folks want to talk with me, they'll call back. Right? Contacts? I have a little wooden box in my desk that holds my card file of people I enjoy contacting from time to time, and it works just fine, thank you. Internet? Good grief, it's EVERYWHERE! I've never pressed that button on my phone and certainly never will. I push the "Clear" button hoping to get rid of everything but the phone, and I get a lady's voice saying something about "Voice Commands". I don't like that lady. Next time I may try to command that she wipe out everything except the phone. Probably worth a try, at least.

I wouldn't necessarily say I have a "love/hate relationship" with my phone. Rather, I feel like a young boy being followed around by a little kid sister with glasses who can't really talk yet.

Ooops! Forgot to apologize. Sorry about that.

A Few Thoughts About Food

Today is grocery shopping day. Five per cent off the total bill at the grocery store. I use a prepared list that I made, based on the layout of the store, to make my rounds. The list may help me keep it down to a gentle roar. Not entirely sure of that, though. Y'see, I do enjoy food! If something looks good, I'll probably toss it into the cart. That makes for some interesting surprises when I get home and unload.

Today they had no fresh cod. Cod is the fish of my forefathers. I bought no fish today. I love cod, not just because my great-grandfather fished it off the coast of northern Norway from about age 12 until he was a grown man, married and moved to the "New World", but because I love the huge flakes and firm texture and taste that's not "fishy". "Next week,", I told the fish monger.

I found the real wild rice again, not "long grain and wild rice" but the wild rice that only Native Americans can gather and sell in Minnesota and Northern Wisconsin. It's really not "rice" at all, but a grass seed of a very special type, and I love the nutty flavor. I found it for the first time last week. Got a box again this week. Can't have too much wild rice around.

Found a little, tiny watermelon, seedless. Cute little thing. I might just keep it around for a while. Ha! I'll have some for dinner tonight with leftover steak and half a baked potato. And red wine.

Got four small, thin pork chops. As a kid, I loved the comic strip "Little Abner" about a guy who lived in the mountains somewhere in the South and ate pork chops. He had a girlfriend, "Daisy Mae". It was probably her that I loved more than him, to be honest. She looked a bit like Penny from the television show "The Big Bang Theory". Daisy Mae wasn't real, just a cartoon. But my Penny is as real as anything. I bet Penny likes pork chops, too. I feel less guilty eating those thin pork chops, even though I have a hankering for those giant honking things that are as large as roasts! Guilt is a great motivator. I was raised Norwegian Lutheran, so I know guilt.

Got some bacon, eggs, and sausage patties (fully cooked, it says right on the package). It's my very first package of sausage since leaving California as a result of the divorce my dear wife wanted. Lots of changes when you are involved in a divorce. Like, for example, I haven't worn my hearing aids since leaving California because I have nobody to nag at me if the television is turned up a bit. ☺ Well, the cat sleeps behind the television. She gets a little ticked off when I turn it on to watch the news. But I get a little ticked off at the news. I figure we're even.

So, my grocery purchases are really pretty normal. Nothing I buy startles the check-out clerks. You don't want to startle check-out clerks. They probably have buttons to push under their counters if you try to buy anything too exotic.

But the Winter Solstice is coming. And then I go a little crazy. I have places in Minnesota where I can buy Scandinavian food. Lefse, lingonberry preserves, Swedish meatballs, cloudberries, sardines, maybe even some reindeer meat (no, not from Santa's eight tiny reindeer), sundbakkles, and other wonderful things. (I will NOT have lutefisk in the house. I'm a good son of Norway, but not THAT good). And I'll have family over for a party, and friends from the old days and the new days here. That party is built around food. Exotic food. And I will sing the Norwegian National Anthem, badly, probably accompanied by my sons who sing it even worse!

Pill Day Today

Today was pill day at my cabin in the mountains. I am eighty-one years of age. If I want to be eighty-two years of age, I have to take pills. It's no small thing, either. Well, some of the pills are small, but some are the size that veterinarians give to horses when horses need pills.

I have four plastic containers. Each container is divided into the seven days of the week, beginning with Sunday and ending with Saturday. Each day of the week is divided into a morning pill place and an evening pill place. That amounts to 56 places to fill. (Somebody check my math on that. I was always a disappointment to my math teachers. Algebra teachers just gave up entirely). It takes me several hours and a bit of cursing to get those 56 places filled with pills.

I take thirteen pills each morning. I take eight pills each evening. Some of those I take both morning and evening. In addition, I have two kinds of pills for pain. One kind I take sort of routinely. The other kind I don't really dare to take. They were prescribed for me out in California, so you can just imagine. But on those few occasions when I do mountain climbing (Hey, I did that last Sunday) I take one of those. They seem to have no effect, other than giving me a sense that I am floating and causing me to forget my own name. One day, if you see me floating by you about three feet in the air, you will know that I took one of those pills.

All the different pills have names. I am not going to go deeply into that because I know how sensitive people can be about names. I am Beaumont Roger Hagebak, for example. My father was Cyril Beaumont Hiram Hagebak. I think my grandmother read entirely too many books. There is a young lady who works at the pharmacy where I get all my pills. Her name is Monalisa. Really! She has an odd sort of smile. Maybe she is on pills for pain like mine? I don't know.

In addition to pills, I have several ointments. I have, for example, Triamcinolone Acetonide Ointment which I am to apply to my skin as needed (I know not what for) except groin, face, underarms, and breasts. That doesn't leave a lot of room. I put some on my ankles once in a while. I also have some ointment to control itching. That's good, because whenever I get the "itch" to go out woman-chasing, I just put on some of that and, presto, the itch is gone!

My doctor just prescribed an ointment that is supposed to increase my energy level. The pharmacist, who I know personally since he gave me my flu shot, put that prescription on "HOLD" until he could talk with me. He said, "That thirty-day supply will cost you $635.17." I said, "I am just a poor old man, living alone with a cat in a cabin in the North Georgia mountains. I don't need energy. I can stick my finger in a light socket if I really feel a need for energy." I did not purchase that medication. I want to leave something to my sons when I pass on. And that is a TRUE STORY. Well, not the part about leaving something to my sons. I'm spending it like any sane American of eighty-one years would!!

So, today was pill day. Something you young "whipper snappers" will have to get used to.

7. Life Can Be A Little Wild In The Woods

Nature's bounty at my door. So many kinds of birds, thieving squirrels, huge pileated woodpeckers, blackbirds that hark back to old Norse mythology. And let's not forget the gentle deer who visit daily, looking for a handout of corn—and the problems involved in hauling corn in the back of the car! A big old bear caught "red handed" stealing the sugar water meant for the hummingbirds. A world of insects: butterflies, carpenter bees, even spiders! These stories barely begin to describe the wonderful creatures that visit this old log cabin.

The Watching Of Birds

I love to watch birds. I feel great when they come to eat out of my bird feeders. But wherever I've lived, the squirrels always seem to get there first. I can easily outsmart deer who are bullying others of their kind. Instead of one pile of corn, I set out three piles of corn about twenty feet apart, and the bully can't manage the distance. Even the smallest deer get fed. And I bought airtight tubs to hold the corn and birdseed I keep in the house, and that (and a guy from Arrow Exterminators) was all it took to outsmart that pesky little mouse who wanted to live in my cabin.

I have never been able to outsmart squirrels, though. However, modern science has now developed a "spicey red hot bird seed". Birds aren't affected by the spiciness. Mammals steer clear of the stuff once they have had a small taste. I tried it for the first time this morning. A squirrel climbed the pole, leaned way out to reach the bird feeder hanging from that pole, took a nice mouthful of seeds, and *smoke started coming out of his ears!!* (Well, not really, but he was spitting out seeds as fast as he could.)

Soon the birds started to arrive, to find that there actually was food for them. My cardinal couple, he of the brilliant red, she of the more subdued tan, even showed up this morning. One or two at a time, it seemed that all the birds in the area came fluttering in for breakfast. The spicy red-hot bird seed costs a bit more than regular bird seed, but it lasts much longer now that the squirrels are dining elsewhere.

I think I will just sit here all morning and watch the birds. It's wash day here at the cabin, but that can wait until afternoon. I have a much more important task to accomplish this morning. I must watch the birds.

The Birds! The Birds!

Quite a few years ago (I lose count) Alfred Hitchcock made a film he called "The Birds", starring Tippi Hendrin, whose mother was a friend of my mother. You can probably still see it late at night on your television set if you can't sleep and want an old-fashioned diversion. The birds finally got their act together and mounted an attack on we humans. I forget who won.

It gets a little bit like that around here, in the half acre or maybe a bit more that I share with my furry and feathered friends in these great North Georgia mountain woodlands. The birds seem to come in bunches at certain times of the day, just like the chocolate loving ladies did when we owned "The Chocolate Express" up in Blue Ridge, Georgia. And children. Musn't forget the children! Interesting, isn't it, how events in life remind you of other life events. But don't let me get sidetracked. This is about birds.

So far, using a wonderful old Reader's Digest book three inches wide and twelve tall named *Book of North American Birds*, I have identified twenty-one species of birds that have set foot and beak on the land I call mine (knowing full well that it belongs to the ages, really). There are the gray Mourning Doves, looking like old English dowagers as they move across the yard searching for some sort of food. There are the Red Shouldered Hawks, who know full well what food they prefer as they patrol high in the air above my trees. The Tufted Titmouse strolls head-first down the big pine nearest my bird feeder, looking for a chance to beat out the White Breasted Nuthatch at the breakfast "table". Northern Cardinals (my Southern friends and family might not realize that this young couple probably was born in the deep South!), him bright red, she a more dignified orange, swoop in for a seed or two. A Pileated Woodpecker chops away on an older oak, not willing to join the crowd at the feeder (and way too large, anyway). His cousin, a Red-Headed Woodpecker, grips the bottom of the feeder and takes a bit more than his share of the seeds inside.

When I step out of the sliding glass door to replenish the hummingbird feeder, the American Crows in the trees above me shout warnings: "Caw, Caw, Caw". Nobody pays them mind. A Blue Jay swings in for a moment to see what all the fuss is about but is soon gone. A Robin walks along, not with the doves but close, looking for his breakfast on (or under) the ground. Chipping Sparrows and Black-Capped Chickadees set up a lively little tune, like musicians playing fancy breakfast music in a resort somewhere. And then...and then...in come the gorgeous American Goldfinches, a guy and his lady, both wearing brilliant yellow outfits this morning. I wasn't expecting them, but there they are, and the crowd gives way to the beauty of this special couple.

There are more of my feathered visitors worthy of mention, but I have run out of both space and time. There are birds that I have not seen yet but may still if I live long enough (oh, and I will) and I wish you were here to share the joy that these little feathered brothers and sisters in life bring to my yard. I really do. Perhaps they come to your yard, too. I hope so.

Just A Simple Bird Feeder

It's a simple bird feeder, really. Square, five inches to a side, and eight inches high. It has a top that hangs over the seed container and looks a bit like a Japanese pagoda or something. The base is kind of a pan that sticks out an inch and a half on each side, and seeds fall down into the pan through slits at the bottom of the container on each of the four sides. If you put too many seeds in the container and it rains, then some of the seeds at the bottom get kind of mildewy. So, you fill the feeder only about a third. The whole thing hangs from a thin wire that runs through a small hole in the top and then up to one of those "shepherd's crooks" that stand in the ground. You can buy them in any bird supply store. The sides are opaque, with a bird design on them. The metal parts are painted fire engine red.

The feeder twists and turns on the thin wire hanger whenever a bird, big or small, lands on its base, giving the birds a panoramic view of their world — my yard. Big birds landing make for bigger twistings, of course, twistings that last longer. I think of a carnival ride for birds whenever one lands and looks around.

Since the landing zone is only about an inch and a half wide, big birds risk life and limb to land on the feeder—but land they do. Well, all but the red-headed woodpecker, the largest bird to have lunch on my feeder. He comes swooping in, grabs the edge of the base firmly, tucks his tail feathers under the whole feeder and, hanging there, pokes his beak into the slit at the bottom of the side he is at and chows down. No other birds land when this big fella is feeding. He doesn't come often, but when he does that feeder is his.

There is a fine-looking couple of cardinals that come to the feeder each and every day, several times a day. The male's red almost matches the red of the feeder. His lady is more of a light tan and orange. He lands first, to make sure all is well, then she arrives. Both find seeds as the feeder swings and sways. They seem to like the sunflower seeds best, fly to a tree to chip the shell from the nut, and then fly back for another.

Smaller birds seem to have developed a pecking order, based primarily on size. If a somewhat larger bird is there, most smaller birds will hang back, perched in nearby trees, waiting for their moment. Some, though, are smart enough to defy the pecking order. The feeder is square, so if a larger bird is on one side, these smart little rascals land on the other side and grab what they can before the larger bird comes around the corner.

On sunny days without rain, this simple bird feeder is in constant use. The cat and I love to watch, although probably for quite different reasons.

And the hummers, with their hanging jar of sugar water about ten feet away, don't seem to care one bit! What goes on at that bird feeder is no concern at all of theirs.

Shadows On The Leaves

Dark shadows in the sunlit trees, swooping high above. Then shadows on the ground, moving fast. "Hawks," I whispered to myself, and grabbed my cane, ready to defend my little family of chipmunks. "No damned hawk is going to hurt my chipmunks!" And then in they came, two of them, virtually identical, to land in a couple of trees in my front yard — one oak, one pine — both birds upright, hanging on the bark. "Those are pileated woodpeckers!! What a gift to me on this day!! Thank you, old Mother Nature, for this wonder of wonders!"

I had not seen a pileated woodpecker since we lived in the Georgia mountains, up near Blue Ridge, and then I saw only one. They are very shy, in spite of their size (up to eighteen inches or more) which makes any sighting unusual and two at a time an unbelievable treat. It's difficult to tell which is male and which is female, since both have similar black and white markings and a bright red crest. The male, though, has an extra stripe of red from his beak along the full side of his head. They love the old forest trees and excavate huge holes in the trunks of those trees, looking for bugs. Ants are particularly prized. This old cabin's grounds are a great habitat for huge black ants!! Back when Europeans first came into these woods, the forests in the east were blanketed by these wonderful woodpeckers, but their numbers died down as their old forest preserves were destroyed to create farms and towns. Today, though, many of those ancient farms are abandoned, lumbering practices have changed, and the pileated woodpeckers are staging a bit of a comeback.

It was a joy to see a pileated woodpecker couple, and to listen to them hammering away at the two old forest trees they had selected. It's less of a joy if you happen to live in a home with a tin roof. The males bang away at the tin, setting up a horrible racket, not to find ants and other bugs but to attract females. I suppose the drummer in a rock band might be doing the same sort of thing. Don't know. I've been a lot of things, but never have been a drummer in a rock band.

A Visit From Messengers Of Odin? (With Apologies To My Sainted Mother)

Today is Wednesday. My Georgia mountain home was visited by three huge blackbirds today. It must have been an omen. I'm of Norwegian ancestry. While most of us have given up our belief in the ancient Norse gods, I've always sort of wondered. Today, because of this odd visit which has never before happened here, I am leaning toward the gods of the Vikings.

That this visit happened on a Wednesday is important. Wednesday is named after "Woden" or "Odin", the king of the Viking gods. Odin is often referred to by students of Viking history as the "Raven God". As King of the gods, Odin had two ravens, "Hugin" and "Munin", who traveled the earth, returning to tell him of all things happening in the world. He is typically pictured with his two ravens, sometimes even four, perched on his shoulders. His ravens are engraved on Viking shields, helmets, banners, and carvings to invoke the power of Odin. When a Viking warrior dies in combat, the "Valkyrie", fierce female warriors who live with the gods, and the ravens of Odin decide which are worthy to enter "Valhalla", the term used for Odin's Hall—a Viking heaven of wine, women, song, and feats of strength.

Perhaps the three huge blackbirds in my trees today were nothing more than three huge blackbirds. But I prefer to think of them as messengers from Odin, here to strengthen my belief in the old gods of my forefathers. Perhaps they were here to check out my qualifications for Valhalla. Quite honestly, I can't see myself playing a harp for all eternity. Being served mead and country-style ribs by beautiful blond Valkyries with long golden braids and songs on their lips holds a lot more appeal for me. Thanks to the three blackbirds who visited on Odin's Day, I'm again leaning toward the gods of the Vikings!

Poem For A Pregnant Doe

The pregnant doe came by today
As every day — too early for my corn
But pregnant does need special care
Before their fawns are born
And so I filled the pan with corn
For this good lady fair
I'd just plopped down to rest a bit
To read in my old chair
When those dark eyes looked into mine
And sought a special share
"I'm going to have a fawn you know
And corn helps me prepare"
She looked at me right through the glass
And says, "Please feed me right away
Before the other six come by
Then I can't eat today"
And so I poured her corn out first
She ate, then walked away
I'm not a Vet (well, Army, yes)
But even I could tell
My little gift of flavored corn
Would help her fawn do well
And you would do the same, my friend
You'd sing as your corn fell"
—Spring, 2017

In the late spring, the pregnant doe gave birth to not just one, but two small fawns. Their mother brought them by the cabin to show me, I really do believe, her little spotted marvels of life. What a delight to see this little family, and to know that the corn helped.

The Breakfast Club

Every morning for the past couple of weeks, three deer have been waiting for me to grab my coffee and plunk down in my recliner to watch the forest world come alive outside. They stand there, looking in at me with those big brown eyes of theirs, asking if breakfast is being served. I have never served breakfast to the deer. At my cabin, we serve only dinner. But there they are, hope springing eternal. And there I am, filled with Norwegian Lutheran guilt—the worst kind of guilt there is. It stays with me even though I'm no longer a Lutheran. Somehow the deer seem to know this. Even worse, I believe the three are a mother and two of her children. She's teaching them how to make use of human guilt in order to get breakfast!

Still watching me, pleading with me, they begin their morning grooming rituals. It's all quite amazing to see. Hind legs are lifted to reach the ears, flicking out whatever it was that got into those ears last night. Mother strolls over and gives one of her children a nice soaking bath with her tongue. The children reciprocate and bathe their mom. They nibble at their own huge black and white tails, taking care of an itch perhaps, or doing damage to a flea. And then all three lie down on the dried oak leaves that cover the yard, all at once, as if there were a command: "Lie down!" Through all of this, though, their eyes track mine, asking, "Where's breakfast?"

I couldn't feed them breakfast this morning if I wanted to. I'm out of corn. Walmart had no more fifty-pound sacks of deer corn when I went shopping yesterday. "Don't know when we'll get more in," said the lady with the badge on her official blue shirt. The deer lie there, watching me, but they're a little too close to the hummingbird feeder this morning. The smallest hummer I've ever seen mounted an attack. He or she was, I'm sure, no more than an inch long. The breakfast club broke up and moved away.

I'll have to find a new place to get my corn today. The dinner club shows up at about 5:30 this evening and there are seven regular members! If there's no corn, they'll eat my shrubs and smaller trees right down to nothing, just out of spite! The restaurant business is no easy life, let me tell you!

Being Just Plain Stupid!

The other day I bought a fifty-pound bag of deer corn (known in the upper Midwest as "cow corn"). Hard yellow kernels. I knew that I couldn't carry a fifty-pound bag of anything. If I ever marry again (perish the thought!) it will have to be to a forty-pound woman who I could actually carry across the threshold. Don't hold your breath. They don't make forty-pound ladies of marrying age. I sure as heck ain't gonna get married again!! I ain't even going to fool around!

Well, I decided to open the top of the bag of corn that was there in the trunk of my car. A few kernels trickled out. No problem. I got a small bucket of corn out of the open bag and fed the deer. Then I had to go somewhere, I forget where. What's worse, though, I forgot the open bag of corn there in the trunk.

The roads here in Lake Arrowhead are curvy and steep, fun to drive. My motorcycling son and his motorcycling seventeen-year old daughter (beautiful, by the way, and still has all her teeth and no tattoos) come to see me just for the thrill of driving these roads. So, I whizzed around, having a grand old time on my way to wherever. I did notice a few kernels of corn down by my feet and vaguely wondered where they'd come from, but I didn't give it much serious thought.

Then I got back home. Opened the trunk. Bright yellow corn all over the trunk, pouring down beside the back seats (I drive a Ford Excitement, I think it's called), pouring onto the floor in the back, pouring under the seats in the front to arrive, finally, at my gas pedal!! I spent over an hour cleaning up deer corn all over my car. And I still couldn't carry the fifty-pound bag!

See what I mean? Being just plain stupid! (Thank goodness I live alone. Nobody else has to know about this!)

A Quandary

The dictionary says that a quandary is a state of uncertainty or perplexity, a dilemma, a predicament. I've been having one of those out in my leaf-covered yard.

Last week, men arrived to plant shrubs and ferns, at a fairly significant dollar cost, in an effort to beautify this old place of mine and improve its value. Most of the shrubs were already half grown, since I may not have the time in this life (no, nothing is seriously wrong with me) to watch smaller plants grow to full maturity. One just never knows. There were a few boxes of small ferns, though, that were planted around the huge stump of the once huge double oak tree near the cabin. The tree had passed on to its reward, and I had to have it cut down a few months ago or run the risk that it might topple over into my huge windows. That would not be a good thing.

The plants were selected because of their beauty, colors, and textures; because of their ability to grow well in a yard shaded by trees all summer; and because they were resistant to the dining habits my little herd of deer. Deer apparently love to have a salad with their meals. Just to be on the safe side, though, I began to feed the deer their corn down by the driveway, quite a little distance from my new plants. "Live and let live" is not nature's way, however.

In the late afternoon, after a fine meal of apple flavored corn, those rascals would decide that a nice salad would be just the thing to add a finishing touch to dinner. They would come up, sniff the deer resistant shrubs, and do a taste test. For most, the tastes were unpleasant. I don't enjoy kale salads, so I understand. The large shrubs suffered no ill effects from the deer. The small ferns planted around the tree stump were not as fortunate. Deer would stroll up to the stump, grip a newly planted fern in their teeth, and yank it out of the ground! Once they had tasted the ferns, though, they dropped them where they stood and walked on. I was left with little baby ferns all over the place, and small holes in the ground around the stump. And me unable to get down on my knees to replace those ferns.

A cane can be a fine thing to own. It can fend off attacks by robbers, keep an old man upright, and even serve as a planting tool. Using my cane, I dragged the baby ferns back to the stump, and poked them into the holes left open by the deer. The problem? Each evening, deer would pull baby ferns out of the ground, do a taste test, and drop them all over again. Each morning I would use my cane to poke the ferns back into those holes. The ferns were beginning to look pretty darn bedraggled!

The quandary? Should I just give up on the ferns, or should I give up on the deer?? I love the deer, and visitors do so enjoy watching them in my yard. But I paid good money for those ferns, and they would eventually hide the stump if allowed to live! I decided to run off the deer.

And so, if some evening you happen to notice an old guy waving a cane and growling like a bear while chasing a herd of deer, you'll know that it's now the deer who are perplexed—in a quandary. I resolved mine. Let them eat corn down by the driveway. No salad!

Innocent Until Proven Guilty? Hmmm ... "Bearly!"

Each morning I slowly and carefully descend the thirteen steps from my lofty bedroom to the ground floor of this old log cabin, and while my coffee is brewing I check on the food just beyond the patio—the birdseed for the birds and the sugar water for the hummingbirds. More often than not in the past few weeks, the hummingbird feeder was empty. I was running through more sugar than a cookie factory just before Christmas.

Then one day I watched as one of my deer (I call them "my deer" but they really belong to no one but themselves) tip the hummingbird feeder up and take a nice long sugar water drink. So, the deer are to blame, says I to myself. I passed judgement on that one particular deer, and whenever she would come near the hummer food, I'd rush out hollering "No" at the top of my lungs! And as if to prove her guilt, she would race off at the sound of my voice. An innocent deer would stick around and try to explain, right?

Well, this morning at about 10:00 a.m., while I am having my morning coffee (I got up a bit late today, it being Sunday and all), up walks a huge black bear! He (I think the bear is male because female bears are a lot smarter than this) assumed a tightrope walker's stance and strolled across the top of the stone wall of my patio to the very spot where the hummingbird feeder pole was placed. He then proceeded to drain the feeder dry. Every last drop!

I opened the sliding glass door and leaped out onto the patio, armed with nothing but my righteous indignation! "And just what the heck to you think you're doing?" I shouted. He turned, gave me one of those "caught in the act" grins, and sauntered off to wherever black bears go when their guilt is overwhelming. I refilled the feeder, made a note to pick up more sugar at the store, and sat down to contemplate the meaning of "justice".

Was the deer innocent? No, but obviously the deer was not solely to blame here. The bear had to shoulder some of the blame, and he had the shoulders for it. There were now *two*, not just one, proven arch-criminals involved. And since the deer go home, wherever that is, at dusk, the bear must be the major culprit in the disappearing sugar water caper after I have gone to bed. I would have to report him to the Lake Arrowhead Security Force folks. Justice must be served—to the bear. I'm not afraid of the deer. I think they're kind of cute. ☺

The Butterflies

The butterflies came by the other day. Some were a deep black color, with maybe a bit of dark purple mixed in. There was one, resting on my stone patio step, that was the softest blue, like the eyes of a Scandinavian princess. Some were orange. A few were maroon. The orange and maroon butterflies stood out clearly against the greenery of spring's middle days. Camouflage is not their strong suit, apparently. I hope they make it until fall, when orange and red leaves on my old oak trees will provide them more protection.

Among the very prettiest were the very light-yellow butterflies, pale, and with wings so delicate you could almost see through them. "Gossamer wings," I thought. They fly by my big windows so very quickly, and in-flight patterns that seem not to be patterns at all: swirling, dipping, scaling new heights, huge aimless circles in the air. Or so it would seem to we groundlings who fly in relatively straight lines, seated in airtight metal tubes that roar through the skies. I love the butterflies. We need more of them to show us how our lives should be lived—with apparent joy and always dressed in our finest.

I once knew a little girl who called them "flutter byes". She was more observant and more correct than the adults who cared for her. That little girl grew up to become one of my lovely adult granddaughters. I hope that she still calls these beautiful creatures by their proper name: "flutter byes"!

Carpenter Bees At 101 Corner Oak Court

If you live someplace where the term "carpenter bee" has never been uttered, you are indeed fortunate. If you live in a brick home, a home made of glass (remember, no stone throwing), or a remodeled steel water tower, you are indeed fortunate. If you live in a log home at 101 Corner Oak Court in the North Georgia mountains, you are one unfortunate mountain man! And that's because a flying bug with a tiny chain saw attached to its rear end loves your home even more than you do.

I had noticed some sawdust here and there on the patio side of the cabin. A couple of small holes in the log siding weren't really a cause for alarm, were they? I sort of stick with the patio side of my home, though, since that's where the deer, the hummingbirds, and the cardinals come to dine. And so, yesterday, when the pest control guy came by to tell me that the other side of my place had more holes than Swiss cheese, I was shocked! That log wall looked like some demented workman with a portable drill had taken out his frustrations on the home I own and love.

For those of you who don't really know much about carpenter bees, let me tell you that those little devils can drill perfect half-inch holes in wood of almost any kind, creating tunnels just wide enough to squeeze their bodies into. They lay eggs at the end of those tunnels. When little carpenter bees are born, they creep to the end of their tunnel, look around, and promise to come back later to drill their own tunnels in almost the same spot. The bees multiply. So do the holes.

The pest control guy allowed as how he could spray some toxic substance on the logs that would solve the problem for me. He already has placed a box filled with toxins at each corner of my home to deal with the mice, and comes by quarterly to spray toxic liquid throughout the inside of my home to deal with the moths, ants, and other low-lifes of the insect world. Small green containers are buried in the ground all around my home to bring toxins to any termites in the area. My little log cabin is beginning to glow in the dark!! But what's a fella to do? I shelled out $375 to have my logs sprayed for carpenter bees. (I am finding that almost anything you need to hire someone to do will cost about $375!)

I can hardly wait until the locusts arrive!

Spiders!

I don't know. Maybe mom was scared by a spider that sat down beside her. Maybe it's the horrible way they capture their prey. I think though, that I don't like spiders (too weak, I HATE spiders), because they have way too many legs. Go to a scary science fiction movie and nine times out of ten the really nasty creatures that we humans eventually defeat have too many legs. Two is good, four is certainly acceptable on deer and other residents of this oak forest who live outside. Sometimes, because of ill fortune, humans wind up with just one leg or no legs at all. They are still just fine. But it they wound up with eight legs, I'd go S-C-R-E-A-M-I-N-G to some other place. And I'd use my cane as a catapult to move me forward faster than the next guy. (All you really have to do to keep from being eaten alive by something with eight legs is to move faster than the other guys!)

When I was going to college, I worked summers as a telephone line-man, climbing poles and digging holes. One morning we were setting up poles alongside a ditch on a country road, and my job was to tamp the loose dirt tight around the poles. Tiring, grunt work. I began to slow down, and the other guys got ahead of me. I quickly finished the job and ran through the ditch to catch up. RAN RIGHT INTO A HUGE SPIDER WEB, POPULATED BY (you guessed it) AN EIGHT-LEGGED HUGE BLACK AND YELLOW SPIDER! There he was, on the front of my shirt! (I sunburn easily, being Norwegian and blond, so I was wearing a shirt even though most of the other guys had taken theirs off to catch a few rays.) In between S-C-R-E-A-M-S I got my heavy-duty work gloves on and batted that thing into next week!! I never run through ditches anymore.

So, I woke up this morning with three spider bites on my right hand, one on my right wrist, and two on my left hand, up near the knuckles. Good grief! I'd been sharing my bed with an EIGHT-LEGGED SPIDER!! I was out of there like a shot! Doing OK now emotionally, but it's 1:00 in the afternoon. I have no idea what I was doing between 7:00 a.m. and 1:00 p.m. Freaking out, I guess. Before this day ends, the exterminator people will be out here, no if's, and's or but's about it! And they better have the correct number of legs!

I love this old log cabin, but there are moments when I'd trade it for a spider-free, modern apartment in a big city. (Not many such moments, though.)

8. This Acre Of Ground And The Visiting Seasons

The yard outside the cabin's three-story windows is the setting for watching the changing seasons of the year. Rain, wind, and violent storms sometimes punctuate the days and nights as the seasons roll on past: summer's muggy days and nights; the gaudy beauty of fall with its colorful leaves and hazardous falling acorns; the dropping temperatures as our winter approaches and then arrives to freeze this world of ours; snowfall, arctic air; and finally spring arrives again.

Trying To Paint A Word Picture

It's early morning. The sun has not yet broken through the trees. A dusky light, though, reveals the patio and yard beyond. You are visiting the old log cabin in the woods, your coffee has been brewed and you are reclining slightly in a large leather chair facing a wall of glass a dozen feet wide and twenty-five feet high that separates the cozy living room from the world outside. You sit inside at this time of day, not wanting to disturb the small feathered birds and the hummers as they begin to arrive for breakfast at the deep red feeders just beyond the stone patio.

Beyond the patio, the land gradually rises. Fifty feet away and off to your left there are huge boulders, piled one on top of another. The boulders are discolored with age, dark gray, and covered with lichens. Oak trees and pines, forty years old and more, grow from the boulder strewn ground. Some have taken root closer to the cabin, twenty feet, ten feet, five feet from the patio. The land beneath them is covered with old dried brown and tan leaves and pine straw. To your right there are some smaller trees and a fire pit standing on a bed of small rocks beside a large, discolored wooden rocker.

As you watch, the sun bursts through from the back of the cabin on your right, and suddenly the tops of the trees brighten into colorful greens and yellows, with light gray branches catching sunlight too. At our level, sunlight moves quickly to the hill of boulders, playing with the grays, the whites, and the light green of the lichens to create a rich mix of brilliance. A chipmunk dashes from his home in the rocks to the other side of the yard, moving almost faster than the eye can follow. A red cardinal, not noticed before the sunlight came through, is perched in a small tree, but leaves to race toward the red bird feeder and his breakfast of sunflower seeds. He's joined by his lady, wearing a coat of light tan and orange. Other birds give way. Two hummers, though, pay no attention as they attack bees that want their sugar water, and perform aerial acrobatics to jealously guard their ownership of the feeder from others of their kind.

And now, as the sun rises above the cabin to shine more directly through the high leaves, the entire yard takes on a dappled appearance—light here, dark shadows there—moving across the fallen leaves and rocks below. Three squirrels creep headfirst down the trunks of the large trees, almost blending into the color of the tree bark. Acorns for breakfast perhaps, or maybe even bird seeds if that old fellow who lives in the cabin doesn't run them off. A beautiful tan and white deer strolls past with her darker spotted baby, followed shortly by a very young male deer with short velvet covered horns, not yet old enough to boast a full rack. A young female follows him through the yard, both looking for corn that isn't there today. The forest will provide this time of year.

Day has come to my home. It's a pleasure to have you visit. Bacon and eggs this morning? With fruit? Toast? Orange juice? Stay right there, this won't take me long.

A Light Rain To Start The Day

Barely heard, there is a soft quiet sort of thunder in the distance this morning. The skies above the cabin have been gray for two days now, off and on, and the mosses and lichens out by the boulders are crying for rain as their color drains from a deep bright green to a pale grayish imitation of their former glory. Having my coffee, I hear what sounds like tiny footsteps on the roof above me, just tiptoes really, as the rain begins to fall.

I get the hummingbird feeder from its bear-safe nighttime refuge in the kitchen sink, run it to the hanger just beyond the patio, and up it goes. Another day has begun, and the little hummers are all over their feeder, in spite of the rain. The other bird feeder, the one with seeds in it, is still full. A squirrel has taken note of that fact and climbs the pole to grab a breakfast of sunflower seeds. I run him off, not once but four times! He finally decides to dine elsewhere, and I've had my exercise for the day.

Something about the rain brings the little chipmunk out from his home deep within the boulders where he is very safe from most predators. He races across the yard through the rain, looking for something good and getting a nice morning shower in the bargain. Then, just as he runs back home, the rain stops. Sunshine and shadows beautify this little world of mine. A glorious morning!

I had been planning to head into town today to order a few meds that I'm running low on, but that can be done tomorrow. It's wash day, and the darks are in the dryer as the whites get a good scrubbing from my washing machine. The trash can has been emptied into a huge truck that comes by weekly, and waits for me to drag it back up the driveway to its place beside my car. My e-mail became unconscious yesterday, and the "One Man Geek" that folks out here use to bring computers back to good health can't come until Monday afternoon. It's going to be an easy sort of day.

I do believe that I'll sit myself down with the list of "Deer Resistant Plants" that I got when attending a short course on gardening in these mountains shortly after arriving here. Fall will be here before too much longer, and this yard needs some new plantings. Nothing that will mess up the forest atmosphere with its leaves, moss and rocks, of course. Just some extra greenery I can plan for. Maybe it will rain some more so I can justify staying home today.

Oh, that darn squirrel just came back! Got to go!

Rain!

I know that it brings the flowers that bloom in May. But, doggone it, it's July! When I was a little tyke and it rained on our Minnesota home, mother used to say, "Rain, rain, go away. Little Bomey wants to play!" (I, the distinguished and white-haired former public health official and university professor, Beaumont R. Hagebak, was "Little Bomey.") I tried it this afternoon, and it didn't work. Maybe it only works for little kids and moms.

Just now the lightning is spectacular. If I were a puppy, I'd go hide under the bed. I may just do that anyway. The lights flicker a little now and then. I keep telling myself that this old log cabin has been here a long, long time, and no little rainstorm is going to affect it much. And then a little voice says, "There's a first time for everything." Where do these voices come from, anyway? I tell myself that if the power goes out before supper time (it used to be dinner time, but I'm "country" now) it would at least be good for my diet. And that little voice says, "What? You're going to let all that food spoil in the refrigerator? Start eating, right now!" The voice is beginning to sound a little bit like my mother.

For almost two weeks now I haven't been able to sit out on my patio. Just as the fancy chairs start to dry, along comes another rainstorm. And I am beginning to worry a bit about the green stuff growing in the cracks between the stones on the patio floor. It looks kind of alive. Moving. Like maybe a science fiction thriller: "The Revenge of the Green Stuff". I wouldn't go out there right now on a bet!

There is a very brave little hummingbird out at the feeder. I can sit here inside and watch him. He's being pelted by raindrops but overcome by hunger he's risking it all to eat. I think I may go and make myself some crackers and cheese. And those cherries I bought yesterday look pretty darn good. Maybe a pork chop sandwich. Or that macaroni salad I was given. There's more than one way to "play", Little Bomey!! More than one way.

Windy Day Today!

It rained last night, and the patter of raindrops on the roof above my bed led me to pull up the covers and scrunch down for a few minutes longer than usual. But duty in the form of "Putih" called so it was shower, shave, shine, and head downstairs to the kitchen to feed the cat that owns me. And to get my morning cup of coffee—let's not forget that!

Sitting there in my recliner with the cat on my lap (oh, yes, she climbs into my lap first thing now, sometimes even skipping her own breakfast, to give me affectionate little "bumps" with her head as I try to keep from spilling that coffee), the clouds give way to a bit of sun on the boulders in my yard. Beautiful, everything so clean and shiny from the washing it all went through last night.

As I watched the hummers and the other birds congregate for breakfast, I realized that the wind was really starting to pick up. The tops of my trees were swaying like so many Hawaiian hula dancers and the birds were darting here and there in unusual landing patterns to grab some seeds.

And then I saw one lone butterfly, one of those yellow-winged little things, moving in a straight line across the yard. Straight lines being more than a bit unusual for butterflies, I was fascinated with the little creature's determination. It was obviously headed for some certain place, and with no time to spare. The wind at six feet above ground was not strong, and my butterfly was making good headway when it decided to ascend to ten feet! Bad decision! The wind took my lone butterfly and blew it back at least twenty feet! As soon as that gust of wind stopped, the butterfly dropped five feet straight down and started across the yard again. This time, it made the trip successfully. I applauded, scaring the cat!

I got to thinking how much like butterflies in the wind our lives so often seem to be. At first, we may flutter around in random patterns, looking into this or that. Eventually, though, we set goals for ourselves and head on out to achieve them. We love, we work in the world, we rise, and we are buffeted by the strong winds of fate. Life is not always easy for any of us. We make whatever adjustments seem to be required to reach our goals, and we move forward once again. You are like that. I am like that. Most of those we love are like that, too. And when there are people who find the winds too strong to cope with, most of us are there to help them through those terribly windy days. The yellow-winged butterfly was alone. You and I are not if we reach out.

The winds here today are left over remnants of Hurricane Harvey that battered the Gulf Coast so fiercely during the past week. No harm came to us in these mountains. The butterfly had to make it across my yard all by itself and did. Those devastated by Hurricane Harvey found that people they never knew were willing to help. Some even put their own lives on the line to rescue others. I applauded the butterfly, but I also applauded the people who helped others on the Gulf Coast. And I applauded those people who knew they needed help and accepted the help of others.

In The Aftermath Of Hurricane Irma

Irma Klatt was my junior high school English teacher in my hometown, Blue Earth, Minnesota. I loved that lady. Used to walk her home after school, or she walked me home, I never really gave that a thought. She was nothing at all like the Irma who devastated the islands, the Keys, and so much of Florida, and then came north to 101 Corner Oak Court as a tropical storm.

It began to rain here, lightly, at 5:00 a.m. on Monday morning. I was sleeping "light", because I'd been watching the storm on my television set and was a bit rattled. I'd been through a few of these things with early responders in the U.S. Public Health Service and knew that the worst was yet to come. All day long the cat and I watched the weather reports. I finally gave up and went to bed at 9:30 p.m. Hadn't been asleep long when I found myself struggling to breathe. My CPAP machine had stopped cold, and I tore off my face mask to get a breath of air. No lights, no power.

Tried to sleep up there in my upstairs bedroom, but it was a "no go". For one thing, I was worried about my big old cat downstairs (she's still afraid to climb the stairs), and what would happen if a tree or two (I have a hundred or more) in my yard were to fall through the huge windows. So, I came downstairs, and got into bed in the "Grandmother's Room", where there's a picture of my mom. When a guy gets a bit rattled, it helps to have a picture of his mom. The cat joined me for all of a minute and a half, left for a while, came back and fell trying to get back on the bed, and never came back again. You may have noticed that cats make up their minds rather quickly. Couldn't sleep there either, and wound up on my recliner in the living room, where I sometimes sleep an afternoon away, cat on my lap. No sleep, but it was kind of nice having a friendly, but equally rattled cat on my lap.

The propane heater on the wall worked wonderfully well, so as the outside temperatures went down, we were still quite comfortable. Of course, the cat has a fur coat. Daylight came, finally. There were NO TREES DOWN! I know, I don't believe it either. Branches, a lot of leaves, but no damage anywhere. A good and kind friend brought me a thermos full of hot coffee—and he's not even Norwegian. What a guy. Breakfast was a small ham sandwich, a previously boiled egg, a bit of fruit, and orange juice—oh, and my morning pills, of course, and hot coffee. I tried not to open the refrigerator any more than necessary, and things appeared to remain edible. (Well, I'm not sick yet.)

I've made a list that includes a Coleman lantern, a Coleman stove, small propane canisters, and more wine. Going to get that stuff, and more, as soon as I can.

Had an appointment with my endocrinologist on Wednesday morning, and my blood pressure was pretty high. I told the young nurse that it probably was because of my trouble sleeping during the storm, but just between you and me, I suspect it was the young nurse. Cute as a bug!

Well! Was That Exciting Or What?!

It had been a quiet little day, sunny, pleasant, low humidity. The bird feeders had been filled early this morning, and the cat and I sat inside watching as our outdoor friends, including the chipmunk, grabbed breakfast. I always make breakfast first for "Putih", the cat, because she then gives me a little lap time. It was beautiful all day. Good thing, too, since I wasn't feeling well at all. I haven't felt "poorly" since I moved here, but today was just a chair-sittin' day.

Then, along about 3:00 in the afternoon, the skies darkened. The birds grabbed their final bites of dinner and headed home. Rain began to fall, gently at first, then increasingly intense, until we couldn't see the trees across the road. We could see our trees, though, and they were swaying back and forth at sixty feet above our cabin. And the rains came down, the cabin roof creating a horrendous lot of noise. Thunder and lightning added to the symphony of sound.

And then the lights blinked out. Briefly, but long enough to interrupt the television news with a message that said that the poor old thing was working hard to get back on. And eventually it did. But only for five minutes, then off again. Its message of hope came on once more. I went to the kitchen to make my humble dinner, and all the appliances that tell time of day (and night) were blinking: "Fix me, fix me, fix me, fix me". I fixed them, then whipped up a dinner of chicken and broccoli in a nice sauce (thanking whatever gods there be for frozen dinners)! Oh, and a salad. And a wee bit of white wine to get my evening pills down.

By the time "America's Got Talent" came back on, the cat and I had eaten our dinners and the thunder and lightning had passed for the moment. "Putih" ("Pootee") came to sit in my lap, just a bit fearful. Those huge windows in the living room seem to bring the outside inside, probably more so to a cat than even to me. There were still rumblings and grumblings and enough rain to please Noah, but at least the trees quit swaying and we didn't have lightning hitting our half-acre. I sat up until the end of the show, way past my bedtime these days, and headed up those thirteen steps to bed. I tried to coax "Putih" to come up the stairs and join me, but so far in our relationship she hasn't built up the courage to climb them—they are open stairs, and I suppose they frighten her. Heck, they even frighten me!

It rained and it thundered all night long. I left the stove light on for "Putih", sort of as a night light, I guess. She ran for her hiding place behind the television set (you can see her white paws back there), and must have stayed there, scared silly, all night long because she hadn't eaten any of the dinner she leaves for a late-night snack, or drank any of her water. She was thrilled to see me in the morning, rolling around on the floor in an ecstasy of affection for the guy who was going to save her from the thunder that was still rolling high above our cabin.

It had been one heck of an exciting night for man and beast (I don't call "Putih" that to her face of course. She has claws.) And we survived it. We both slept a bit this afternoon, though.

Summertime ... And The Livin' Is Muggy

June was an absolute delight up at the cabin in the woods, cool, no humidity, few biting insects. Of course, that's the time I chose to leave for my summer vacation in Minnesota, North Dakota, and Wisconsin, where (goodness knows) it could have snowed! (It didn't!) And now, in mid-July, summertime has come to Georgia with a vengeance. It always has, always does, so we Georgians learn to deal with it. I've lived here over 40 years, and I'm still alive (mostly).

Summertime in Georgia can be a wonderful time. You get your outside chores done early so that you can sit back in an old rockin' chair on the porch and sip mint julips in the afternoon. And since mint julips are basically bourbon, some sugar, some fresh-picked mint leaves (stems on), and ice, you usually are ready for bed by 3:00 or so in the afternoon. You sleep through the heat. Get up early the next mornin' and do it all over again.

Today, though, I had to go to town. I haven't worn my hearing aids since I moved back to Georgia because here, people talk slow. But my hair was getting in the way of my hearing, so the first order of business was to get a haircut. Then, since I want to be well thought of, I went to the cleaners with umpteen shirts and one pair of pants. (Shirts have to be changed a lot, but a man can wear a pair of pants almost forever!) Got some more of that special "hot" birdseed that keeps the deer away (the squirrels, though, are crazy for the stuff!). Got gas, got my medications (I don't need to eat breakfast, since I have enough meds to make me feel full all day) and then went grocery shopping. MAJOR ERROR!

It was after noon when I left the grocery store. The young man who helped me to the car with my groceries melted, right there in front of me. I got into the car by grasping the door handle with a used handkerchief—not too sanitary, I suppose, but it got the job done. Avoid opening the driver's side door for a few days without disposable rubber gloves. And I drove home to my little log cabin in the woods. Then I had to carry the groceries in, during the heat of the day! Except for the fact that I had quite a bit of frozen stuff (I dine well on the nights I have with Marie—Marie Callender) I could have just let it all sit there in the car, wine bottles popping open with the heat. Instead I made four trips. As my sainted mother would have said, "Uffda!".

I chilled the white wine immediately. I mean, NOW! My energy level is "zip" (an actual measurement used in making men's pants), and I just want to quit this crazy writing thing and get me a mint julep started. But I haven't had bourbon in the house for years because it makes me just plain stupid. So I think I'll have a glass of wine inside the cabin, looking out. No birds, no hummers, no squirrels, no nothing moving out there.

Guess they found out about mint julips, too. Or fermented grapes. I sure hope so. We all need something to deal with "muggy" in these wonderful Georgia summers.

But at least the cotton is high. (And fish are jumpin', too.)

There's Something Very Special About Fall

Spring certainly has its charms. Announced by daffodils, it comes along all too slowly after a cold and dark winter. But winter has its moments, too. Here the air becomes brisk and free of the humidity that summer brings. And summer, ah. A time to relax, under an umbrella on a lawn chair, sipping a tall glass of something or other and thinking slow, easy thoughts. But fall! Delightful, colorful, dancing in the leaves fall! What a grand time, perhaps the grandest of all!

Today, Lake Arrowhead was adorned with color—reds, oranges, yellows—shouting to those of us willing to hear that fall had arrived at last! A circus! And we all have front row seats! Leaves fell from the oaks to litter the ground so beautifully that there was no thought of raking. The chipmunk scampered from one tree to another, searching for acorns and such for his winter larder. The hummers have left for warmer places, and there seem to be fewer birds as well, so those who have stayed behind have unfettered use of the feeder hanging by the patio. A short drive past the smaller lake to get the mail was simply grand, as the colors of fall were reflected in the water all along the shore. A bright fall sun added to the glory of it all. It was a great day to be in North Georgia.

This old log cabin has no grassy front yard, so rakes are unnecessary here. Unwelcome, even. But I do recall my childhood in Minnesota when dad would rake leaves into a huge pile that my sister, our neighborhood friends, and I could jump into! Better than those new-fangled trampolines, for sure. And later, when the raking chores fell to me, the leaf pile in the back yard was where we teenagers would congregate with hot dogs on sticks, to dine on with the beans, potato salad, and kool aid that mother would bring out to us. Later in the evening we toasted marshmallows for dessert. Joyous recollections of a time past, and a wish from deep in the heart that our grandchildren could know the fun that fall's leaves brought. Friendships were forged in those leafy backyard fires of fall.

As I think and write, my big old cat lies on the carpet enjoying the sun streaming into the living room through the huge windows this cabin has to bring our forested world indoors. She looks at the falling leaves, at the few remaining birds flitting past, and thinks her own thoughts. I think that they are much like my own, perhaps. Old men and old cats probably think quite a bit alike, particularly in the fall. Tasks planned for have all been accomplished. Some holiday packages arrived to help me dress up this old place in finer garb, and to spread some joy among family members when the holidays arrive. A new set of gas fireplace logs has been ordered, with a remote that won't require me to get down on my knees to light the fire. They will be installed later this month. It has been an unusually good day at 101 Corner Oak Court.

We hope that your day has been unusually good, too. Fall is here, you know. Enjoy! Dance!

The Falling Leaves ...

This old cabin has windows that are twelve feet wide and go up two and a half stories to the very peak of the roof above. As with most things, there's good and bad about that. The bad comes on very cold nights when the windows offer little in the way of protecting the warmth in the cabin. The good, though, outweighs the bad on a day like this one when the leaves come spiraling down.

Never before, at least that I can remember, have I been able to see a leaf fall from a sixty or seventy-foot tall tree located just twenty feet from my windows—and watch the journey from the top of the tree to the ground so far below. It's really quite a thing to see. When the breeze is soft, almost still, a single leaf says, "So long!" to its brothers, and begins its descent alone. But when the day is windy, a gust assaults the trees and hundreds of leaves fall at the same time. Now that is spectacular! The cat and I both watch, absolutely fascinated by the spectacle. It's like watching a team of parachutists leaping from an airplane and swirling down to a soft landing far below.

The blower comes out of its spot near the back door, and the cat dashes for cover. It's a noisy contraption, but it gets the job done. I had to clear the path from the driveway where my Ford is parked to the patio, because the covering of leaves made it seem like no path at all. While I was at it, I also blew leaves off the patio, clearing that space so the cat can get hugely excited when a bird or chipmunk comes close to the windows. She's a house cat, never been outside, never dared to go, but she still has those predatory instincts. I suppose I do too, but small birds and chipmunks just aren't my thing.

So now the yard is covered with brown leaves, attractive in their own way. Soon I'll be raking them away from spaces where summer sun leaves the ground bare, and I'll be putting in pine straw there to cover. But for now, let's just enjoy those leaves and the rustic look they provide to this old place of mine. There are still a few, still green but changing, to add to the yard before I rake.

Mighty Oaks From Little Acorns Grow

If you live in a log cabin in an oak forest, and pay attention, you learn a lot about life.

September is the time of year when oak trees drop acorns. It's also the time of year when deer choose acorns over field corn for dinner. It's also a time of year when living in a log cabin under a bunch of oak trees can be an experience. You see, oak trees, like most life forms on this old Earth of ours, seek to propagate their kind. For an oak tree, that means growing acorns high in their branches and dropping them to the ground in the hope (Do oak trees hope? I think so.) that some will land in just the perfect spot to promote their own growth into mighty oaks, too.

What this means, of course, to humans and cats living in oak forests ("ping!!") is that we risk our own lives in September ("pong!!"). The cat settles into my rather ample lap for a bit of petting as I sip my morning coffee ("pang!!) as acorns fall on the roof high above our heads. They fall like there is no tomorrow ("ding!!") and we leap a foot in the air from a sitting position! This cat, in order to leap that high, must use her claws! ("pank!") She is seated on my lap. You begin to get the picture. Unlike the oak trees, I can't have more children now, since September came rolling around! The cat has seen to that ("donk"!!).

Once an acorn landed inside the chimney ("bang...rattle, rattle... ping!!"). I now am certain that there is a metal flu in the chimney somewhere, sort of an acorn barrier. I heard it.

I have put up a sign down by the driveway entrance ("boing!!") that says, "This is a hard hat zone." I do have umbrella insurance (yes, that's what they call it) on this place to protect my great wealth if some visitor should fall or something, but the umbrella policy may not be strong enough to protect against falling ("bing!!") acorns! The insurance people would call it an "act of God" although no one has yet been able to explain ("ping!!") to me why God would want to have acorns hitting people on the head! I'm no theologian, but you'd think that ("ding!!") God would want acorns to fall on fertile soil so as to create more acorns, wouldn't you? My head is not very fertile, although there is a lot of crap in it that might be considered fertilizer, I suppose.

I do worry about the little forest ("pang!!") creatures who share this forest with me. I haven't seen the chipmunk for several days. The hummers are fast enough to ("boink!!") dodge acorns as they fall (I've seen them do it, and it's impressive), but the other birds, what about them? The deer seem to have developed an immunity to falling ("pank!!") acorns. Thick skulls, probably. There were two male foxes killed by neighbors this past week. The foxes ("zing!!") were running around, howling, and coming right up to people. Folks thought they were rabid. ("Pong!!") I think the acorns were at fault. The foxes were trying to tell us, "The sky is falling! The sky is falling!" And look what they got for their trouble. But they aren't eating acorns anymore, are they? (Part of the oak tree's Master Plan.)

So, I have learned that life begets life or, if you are an oak tree, tries to beget life, very powerfully. And I have learned that begetting, for humans, requires that the cat on your lap be declawed. I have learned that God must be very confused about life. I know I am. ("ding!!") And I have learned that life requires that you avoid running around yelling, "The sky is falling!!" Way too risky if you value your own life. I've learned a lot about life this September. ("donk!!")

A Rather Brisk Night!

It's late October, true. But this is Georgia, not Minnesota! The outside temperature got down to the mid-30's (Fahrenheit) last night here on Corner Oak Court.

As a dreary, dark old day gave way to a dreary cold old night, the temperatures plummeted. Here in the cabin, I'm not sure that the ancient "auxiliary heating unit" in the crawl space ever recovered from the three-hour power outage the night before. There was a strong wind blowing the leaves around on the patio, a very chilly strong wind, and that wind found every opening to the inside far better than even our little field mice could! The living room with its two and a half story windows got to be a bit too cool, even for the cat. I cranked up the thermostat to 84, but it never got to more than 71 degrees on that thermostat's wall, so the living room was probably in the fifties! Bedtime came earlier than usual.

This morning the upstairs bathroom in my private "suite" was too cold to consider a shower, or even a shave. I just combed my hair, put on some clean undies, brushed my teeth, and took this poor old body downstairs for my morning coffee. The sun came up and so did the outside temperature, as I sat with a blanket and a warm cat, sipping that coffee. By noon, a walk to the car seemed almost possible. The television people told me that we would hit the mid-sixties today and get as warm as the high seventies later in the week.

Yes, friends and family in Minnesota, in Fargo, and in Wisconsin, I have become a weather wimp. In some ways, I admire your bravery in the face of winter sleet and snow and I chuckle to myself when I recall "trick or treating" on Halloween with snow coming down while wearing full winter gear under my old sheet ghost costume. And I do hear you laughing at me for complaining about temperatures in the mid-thirties. But I'll get even with you in February, and don't you forget it!

The guy from the propane gas company is coming Thursday to fix my fireplace. So there!

Fall Has Fallen

A nostalgic morning.

I'd reset the thermostat from cooling to heat last night before bed, since the world outside was already cooling down quite a bit. It was good to hear the heat come on, and to know that the cat and I would wake up to a warm cabin this morning. It was predicted to be cool outside, finally!

Sleep was a bit difficult. I'd been reading some of Stephen King's work, and his horrifying imagery floated through my mind as I tossed and turned. Eventually, though, I slept. Rain pattered on the roof above my head all night long.

Got up this morning and went through my little clean-up rituals, put on a warm shirt, and came down the stairs, cane in one hand, railing in the other, noticing that the window above the stairs was steamed over. When I got downstairs, I was stunned to see that all the windows were steamed over! The cat and I could see out only at the corners where the fit wasn't as tight as it probably should have been. An hour later the windows were still steamed over! Cold air outside, warm air and moisture inside, quite a combination.

The film of moisture was on the inside of my windows, and I was reminded of my childhood in Minnesota. In the early fall dad would climb a ladder to each window in our home, remove the screens which had been put on for summer, wash the windows, and then attach the heavy storm windows which had been stacked in a corner of the basement since spring. He'd turn the radio up high to listen to University of Minnesota football as he worked his way around the house. When I got old enough, I would hand him up the storm windows and hose off the screens that would soon be stored in the basement for the winter.

And then we would wait, my kid sister and me. Eventually it would be so cold that frost would form on the windows inside the house. "Jack Frost came by last night", mother would say. Jack Frost left stunning patterns on each window, all different, all beautiful. You could see castles, and flowers, and all sorts of things in the frosted glass using the eye of your imagination. And most fun of all, you could make baby feet on the windows.

Baby feet? Yup! You make your hand into a loose fist. You press the side of your hand opposite your thumb up to the frost and hold it there a moment. There on the window is the imprint of a baby foot. Then you hold the tip of your finger to the end of that imprint five times to make toes — the end away from the heel, of course. By golly, it's a baby footprint! You could make a bunch of them alternating your closed fists, and it looked like a baby had walked right up the window!

I made some baby footprints this morning. A trip back in time for me. Maybe it could be for you, too. Fall has come to my cabin in the woods, my arthritis has become less painful, and I have become years younger, making baby footprints on my windows. Try it sometime.

All Right, So I'm A Wimp

Back in an April in the early 1970's, there were still three feet of snow, maybe more, on the little Lake Superior town of Ashland, Wisconsin, home of Northland College, where I served as the Dean. The snow was sooty black on top because most homes and businesses burned coal. I had been contacted by a physician heading up a health district in western Georgia, suggesting that I bring my wife and come South for a visit and interview. Governor Carter and his wife, Rosalyn, were building a community mental health network throughout Georgia, and I was being tapped to help.

Our plane landed in Atlanta, where we were met by a fellow who drove us on a partially completed Interstate Highway to LaGrange. Red clover was growing in the median, and I asked our driver to pull over. We picked some wild red clover, felt the warm spring air, and became Georgians in those moments by the side of the highway. When we returned home, we packed up our things, sold our 100-year old home, bid farewell to friends and family still living in cold country, and headed for warmer climes. I haven't been back in the winter since.

This morning the outside temperature at 8:00 was eighteen degrees, not including wind chill. The new plants that were professionally installed shortly after Christmas were probably digging their little roots as deep and fast as they possibly could. The small birds at the feeder were twice their normal size, fluffing out their feathers to insulate themselves against the cold. The new suet log, now hanging from a tall shepherd's hook in the front yard and filled with seed-pocked peanut butter suet, was a great hit for their breakfast this morning. Given to me by close friends from California, that suet log was probably saving lives as that outside temperature stayed well below our local "average". Two squirrels kept me busy this morning, chasing them off the bird feeder. They were eating spicy "hot" birdseed that should have kept them at bay (birds have no taste buds so spicy means nothing to them). There still are acorns littering the ground all around this cabin in the woods, so I don't feel too guilty about yelling at squirrels.

I'll probably stay home all day today. Plenty of food, just enough red wine for another day, and the gas heater on the dining room wall throws out heat at a fantastic rate. I've got this cat, too. She's warm, and in weather like this she's a demanding lap-sitter. Made myself a nice, warm breakfast, took my pills, and am now preparing to work on my two projects for the day: loading up my daily/weekly/ morning/evening pill containers, and writing checks to pay for all the stuff I got last month on VISA. I can sit at the dining room table, facing that wall space heater, and be just "toasty", thank you!

My friends in Minnesota, where I was born and raised (except for a three-year sojourn with the Sioux Nation in South Dakota as a child during World War II), are probably bundling up for an afternoon of snowmobiling, maybe even skiing, and shouting their joy about the cold weather at the top of their lungs! Me...I am a self-proclaimed wimp! At eighteen degrees, the great outdoors hold no charms for me. I'm an indoor guy, living with an indoor cat, and maybe even with some indoor mice. And I know that it will warm up out there well before April.

The First Snowfall!

It's coming down pretty good right now, my first snowfall since moving into this old log cabin last February. Here in Georgia it's known as an "early snowfall", coming through on December 8. In Minnesota, the state of my birth, childhood and youth, an "early snowfall" might be in September, and by Halloween the kids are wearing winter gear under their ghostly sheets.

The outdoor temperature this morning is about 35 degrees Fahrenheit, so the snow is not sticking to the roadways or the roof of my cabin. They are just wet for now, but tonight when the temperatures plummet, the roads will become treacherous. Some of the bridges are pretty scary already. Later in the day I will have to drive to town because I'm out of food for the deer—proving once again that procrastination may not be the best life choice. But the deer need that apple-flavored corn more today than any other day in the past month and I'm one of their suppliers. Day before yesterday there were two large four point bucks in the yard, and last evening an adolescent guy with two horns atop his head like five inch sticks of wood trotted up to my feeders. The "ladies" let those big bucks eat their fill, but the arrogant bucks often allow the little yearlings to have dinner with them. I like it when that happens.

The snow is sticking to the fallen leaves and boulders that make up my front yard, and to the trees as far as the eye can see. The world is turning ever more white, and quiet. Even the huge trucks that rumble past with concrete to pour or trash to haul aren't making the usual noise. The stone patio is turning white as I sit here and write. I've plugged in the decorated tree, and the spirit of the holiday is overwhelming me. The gas logs are burning brightly in the old stone fireplace, and I feel that Santa could walk through the door any time now.

The cat, "Putih", is something to behold this morning. Usually, I make my coffee and her breakfast, sit down in the recliner, and watch as the world outside those huge windows comes to life. She leaps up on my lap, content to stay there and purr for twenty minutes or more. This morning, though, she leaped to my lap to say, "Good morning, Poppa," stayed all of two minutes, and was gone to watch the snow come down at the big windows. She occasionally swung by to tell me about the snow, and probably ask what the heck was going on. I try to tell her, but I still don't speak "cat" terribly well. Then she's back at the windows to watch again.

This is the "sticky" kind of snow. It sticks to stuff. The trees are all taking on a blanket of white that is making them absolutely beautiful even without their colorful fall leaves. If there were enough of it, I could make a snowman or maybe even a fort out in the yard. Right now, I could go out there and lie down on my back, and move my arms up and down, and make an angel! I'm taking pictures instead but can't seem to get them loaded into my computer this morning. So typical of me—a poet, a dreamer, and not one bit of technology in my entire system.

It's snowing so hard just now that I can see only about a city block before the world out there turns totally white. The world is just me, my black cat, and my old cabin. Just for now, I sort of like it that way. I'm betting that you would, too. A day for resting and remembering snows so long ago, so far away, so very beautiful.

Thoughts On A Foggy Mountain Morning

The sun usually wakes me up at around 7:15 each morning as it peers through my bedroom windows and lights up the room on the second floor. It didn't get the job done this morning though. My old internal alarm woke me at that early hour. Up and at 'em! All shaved and shined and ready for the day, downstairs I went. First order of business: feed the cat and make myself a cup of coffee. Then I can sit down in my recliner.

The cat leaps up and meows a hearty "Good morning, dad!" I scratch her head a bit and check on the world outside those big windows.

This morning that outside world was very quiet. Not even a bird flitting through the trees for breakfast at the feeder. It was impossible to see across the road because we were "socked in" with an early morning fog. The cat went to sit in front of the windows, and gave out a plaintive "meow", telling me it was just too quiet out there to suit her. I kind of liked it. It added to the cozy feel of the fireplace. All alone in a world of fog, dark trees rising into an unseen sky, and the newly planted ferns and bushes looking green and healthy as they began to sink their roots into the soil.

Ordinarily the cat and I sit together and enjoy the sunrise as the first rays of morning hit the very tops of the trees across the road. I finish my coffee as the sun works its way into my front yard, waking birds and small creatures of one kind or another. The patio remains dark through the morning, brightening only as the sun gets high enough in the sky to overcome the shadow cast by the cabin. But this morning there was no sunshine—just a gradual brightening of the white fog surrounding us.

As much as I love the sunshine on my home and yard for the warmth it brings this chilly time of year, a morning with heavy fog can be wonderful too. Perhaps it's the variety that I enjoy most. These mountains offer variety in abundance. Plant and animal life of all kinds find a home here. So do people from former homes near and far away, like myself, who quickly learn to appreciate the varied gifts of personality and belief that the others bring.

Last week we had ten inches of fresh, new snow on the ground in this community of ours. Then we had sun, and the snow was all but gone in two days. Today we have a morning fog, and tomorrow my new plants look forward to the promise of rain. Then a few days of sunshine are predicted again. Variety, they say, is the spice of life. Bring it on, I say. The spicier the better!

Arctic Air

It was minus 36 degrees at International Falls, Minnesota. That's 68 degrees below freezing!!

Here at the cabin, it was in the 20's outside, and just 62 degrees inside when I got out of bed. The cat was yelling at me: "Meow, meow, meow, dammit!!" and this time I knew what she was saying. "Get down here and crank up the space heater, you old fool!"

My furnace doesn't quite cut it when the temperature falls below, say, 40 degrees outside. The air coming through the floor registers has a kind of cool feel to it, like it's a struggle to push hot air all the way from the furnace at the back of the house to the living room at the front. The ducts are insulated, but that doesn't seem to help much. And when arctic air hits 101 Corner Oak Court, forget it! If it weren't for that gas space heater on the dining room wall, and the artificial logs (I'm not supposed to say "fake" since that word is being overused by politicians these days), the cat and I would be frozen lumps of protoplasm—and she has a fur coat!

On mornings like this one, I don't shower and shave first thing. Instead, I put on my big old dark blue robe, a heavy, thick masterpiece of the cloth maker's art, and my new slippers, and creep down the stairs to make my cup of coffee and feed breakfast to "Putih". I've gotten so good at it that both of those tasks are completed at precisely the same time. I crank up the heater, turn on the fireplace, and plunk myself down in my recliner. The cat runs over just as I sit down (one day she's going to wind up "squished" if she's not careful), leaps into my lap and, with her claws, digs herself a spot to sit on my robe. There we sit, waiting for the cabin to warm up.

I have friends up in Minnesota who sit naked in basement saunas* this time of year, and then, still naked as a flock of jaybirds, run outside and roll in the snow! These are, obviously, crazy people. Everyone should have a few crazy friends, though, to compare themselves with. If you don't do this sauna thing in the midst of winter, you must be mentally healthy—correct? Sure.

Well, all this to say that it's "hunker down time" in the North Georgia mountains. I'm not looking forward to my propane gas bill this month, but at least I'll be warm enough to read it. The sun is up this morning, and it's a beautiful day out there. I don't let that fool me. The temperature may get to 30 degrees later in the day. Arctic air. You can't see it, but you sure can feel it. Even in Georgia where, as the Bible says, "Many are cold but few are frozen." Something like that.

A sauna is a little tiny knotty pine-lined room in the basement with a wooden bench, well sanded so you don't get slivers in awkward places, and a powerful heater upon which you throw cold water from time to time to make steam. It has a door that allows you to run outside and roll naked in the snow when the spirit moves you. It is not sexy. It does cure blackheads and boils and claustrophobia, however.

Stories Of Spring

Spring came to the log cabin in the woods, according to the calendar I have here, on March 20, 2018. Bat crap!

Spring is hiding somewhere, possibly down in Key West, drinking Jamaican rum with its cell phone turned off. Also, on March 20, I had an appointment for another round of tests—this time checking up on the workings of my esophagus—and I was to turn my body over to those white-coated medical testers by 8:00 a.m. The temperature outside as my home health aide and I got into my car to make this wintry trek was twenty-seven degrees Fahrenheit! Twenty-seven degrees! It was still dark, too. I've seen better springs on $35.00 flop house mattresses!

As we drove south toward the chamber of horrors that medical people call "Imaging", the car slowly warmed up and so did we. I warmed up more quickly since my home health aide has to drive, and the cold steering wheel is pretty difficult to overcome during the first twenty miles or so, even with the heater registering "HI" (which doesn't, in car talk, mean "HELLO"). She's paid for her cold hands though, and her warm heart, so I don't feel too much old-fashioned Norwegian Lutheran guilt. Just enough to make my old Norwegian mother smile.

A week or so earlier, the flowering trees had flowered. Whites, and some delicate pinks, brightened the woodlands I now call home. I figured that those lovely little flowers would be littering the ground everywhere. On closer inspection, I found that they were frozen to the trees! Still colorful, though. The water that I set out for the birds had gone from liquid to solid. A lone squirrel was chowing down at the bird feeder on special birdseed that had been so spiced up at the bird seed factory that only a bird without taste buds could enjoy it. To that squirrel, the stuff was like hot sauce on a pulled pork barbeque! On a normal spring day (whatever that is) he would have been gasping and wheezing and spitting like crazy. This first day of spring 2018, his eyes watered just a wee bit.

As for me, we got to the "Imaging" place, and I stripped to the waist before they tied one of those "open in the back" gowns on my poor old frame. I then was forced to stand on a small platform, with my back (remember, it's "open in the back") against the coldest piece of metal in the universe. They gave me a large cup filled with, I think, ground up chalk taken from chalkboards in elementary schools all across Georgia. Vile stuff! I told the physician in charge that the addition of a bit of vodka would make it more palatable. He laughed. Normally, I like laughing physicians. It's the serious ones you have to watch out for. Not this time. I disliked this one with a level of dislike I had reserved only for my Drill Sergeant in Basic Military Training so many, many years ago. Lived through it, though: Basic Training AND Imaging.

Spring 2018 has come to Georgia. A frigid, vile tasting day that will live in infamy. And we saw our first mosquito!

9. The Holidays At The Cabin In The Woods

When you live alone you probably get more excited, sooner, about the holidays than other folks. You buy the essentials and then some. You recall past holidays with both joy and sadness. Your artificial tree finally arrives in a big intimidating box. The tree gets decorated though, and friends come by. Holiday greeting cards are sent, and then you finally find some time to reminisce about holidays long passed as you enjoy the goodies brought to the cabin by the wonderful ladies who live in this neighborhood. Then the New Year dawns, bound to be different than this one. And so you "resolve" with resolutions that are likely to be broken by February.

It's Not Too Early To Be Thinking About The Holidays, Is It?

I'm finding that when you live alone you get out there ahead of most folks when it comes to the holidays. Had my holiday cards made in September. About a hundred and twenty all addressed, too. It's now early November and my gift list is complete, and most are purchased and on their way from the big Amazon store in the sky. Now it's time to consider how this old cabin will be decorated for the season.

Need to get a fake tree because attaching all those little lights to a real tree every year is, to me at least, a pain in the posterior. I want one of those tall, full but skinny ones, that will fit by the sliding glass door. I'll need to send off for a bunch of Norwegian straw ornaments. I already have the big straw goat if the mice haven't eaten it yet out in the shed. He'll stand over on the file by the computer, I think, surrounded by greenery. Three of those fancy candles, a couple red ones and a tall, skinny white one, would be nice. One red one for the "coffee table" (which is actually an old sea chest), another red one for the dining room table, and the tall, skinny white one for the top of the antique desk—all surrounded by greenery, of course.

The greenery should be real evergreen boughs and pieces, if at all possible. I'll need a long string of the stuff to climb the stair railing from the main floor to my second-floor art studio. Another long string would look nice on the mantle, woven into the many artifacts that represent my life and times, my "reminiscing" stuff. Some greens would dress up the antique kitchen clock on the wall in the dining room. Oh, and an evergreen wreath for the door on the side of the cabin that everyone but me thinks is my front door. They think that because it's closest to the driveway where guests park their cars, but the real front door is in the glass wall by the patio that looks out on the leaf-strewn yard with its boulders and its trees.

I've already got a nice new tablecloth for the dining room table, red with fancy gold circles on it. Still have a lot to buy, though. That may be about as far as I'll go with the list I've made for this year, and I'll save the decorating of the two guest bedrooms and the upstairs for 2018. My health has really been pretty good, so the holidays in 2018 are a good possibility.

I'm hoping to have friends over for a few Norwegian delicacies: lefse (sort of a very thin potato pancake), some lingonberry and cloudberry preserves, a few of those little sardines, some Norskie holiday cookies, Scandinavian cheeses, flatbrod, salty licorice, and stuff like that. As a concession to the modern American palate, I'll also have some crackers, meats, shrimp, and some good old Minnesota wild rice.

I found Minnesota wild rice in the local Publix last week and went to find the manager to tell her how pleased I was to have available in Georgia some of the food from my childhood in Minnesota. Just wild rice, with a bit of boiled onion for flavor. None of that fancy white or brown rice at all. The only problem I foresee is that some folks are going to be put off a bit by my boiled wild rice. When it's boiled, those little black rice kernels look way too much like mouse droppings.

The Season Approaches, Whether We Want It To Or Not...

I'm sure it's been said before, this can be a tough time of year for some people. I've kept myself busy all day getting ready for the Norwegian Christmas Party I'm having on December 10. The menu is all set, and even the Swedish meatballs (made by, not of, Swedes, contrary to rumor) have been purchased. Still have to get shrimp, of course. And all the imports from Norway are due here at the cabin in two days now. I've got little party favors for the families who show up, meaningful ones that will protect their households for the coming year and longer if one believes in gnomes. I've unpacked my mother's good silver and her fancy dishes for all the foods (guests will eat off plastic to save wear and tear on the dishwasher, but what the heck, that's to be expected, right?) So, I have things pretty much in order, ahead of the game as they say.

I've even made up some little cards for the table to tell people what they are eating, and in some cases how to eat whatever it is. I was a Federal bureaucrat for quite a few years, and so I'm good at this sort of thing. Instructional devices are very important. And I am ready!

That, of course, gives me a bit of time to sit and think about Christmases past. Probably not a great idea. Since the cards went out, I've gotten a number of phone calls from friends and relatives who didn't know I was living alone in this log cabin. My "Best Man" at our wedding called, and we talked a long time. A fellow in Minnesota who had me serve as his "Best Man" called, to insist that he was the "best man" in the room at the time. I didn't argue the point. Came close to tears at each phone call, because I am not the stoic Norwegian of fable and verse. I'm kind of wimpy, to tell the truth, when it comes to deeply personal matters. But it is wonderful to have such friends. They are my real treasure, and my IRA pales by comparison.

So, it's raining now, which really helps the "sorry for myself" mood along. But friends from Minnesota send me photos of blizzards up there today, and that does make me feel some better. Their snow falls sideways in strong winds. My leaves do. I'm not sure I could handle a Minnesota winter anymore. But many of my Christmas memories have to do with snow, and when I was a child I used to worry if there wasn't snow by mid-December. How would Santa ever get his sleigh going without snow? You know? He always did. And ate the cookie and drank the milk, too.

I'm lonesome for my mom and dad, and for my sister (born two years and one day after me, I used to tell her that she was the worst birthday present I ever got, and a day late). I'm lonesome for a time that doesn't exist anymore, when an orange in the bottom of the stocking hung by the chimney with care was an exciting thing to receive. I have many good friends today, and love them dearly, but I am lonesome for those who have passed on out of this life. I miss some old Army buddies who spent their Christmas with me years ago. High school and college friends, all held close in my heart and in my mind. Long ago sweethearts are missed, too. It's a time for thinking of and remembering all those wonderful people that made my life such a grand thing.

And so the season approaches. And while I no longer practice the faith of my fathers, and believe that the Winter Solstice has powerful meaning for the season, I miss the joy of my youth at this time of year and the fact that I once even believed in Santa Claus. I'm hoping to actually see him this year! Bet I will, too. And I hope you do, also. Blessings as this time of hope approaches.

Another Strange Set Of Experiences ...

Well, there I was, cooking up a nice set of baby back ribs in my oven. Yes, if you do it right, you can make them taste just as good as the outdoor kind. So, I lean over to check the ribs and out of my shirt pocket falls my cell phone...INTO THE OVEN! I grabbed my tongs, but the phone slipped out of their grasp. I finally had to get a cooking fork thingy and drag the phone over to the side where I could grab it with a bigger set of tongs and toss it onto the counter. Uffda. It has a huge scar, but it still works. Unreal. The ribs were tasty, though.

Then, looking in my huge closet, for a box with some holiday ornaments maybe, I found a letter from my dad when I was a soldier in the U.S. Army, Germany Occupation Force, telling me that he and mom had gotten closer to my high school girlfriend and thought she was a "very fine young woman". Agreed. She and Andy were married three days after I was discharged! ☺ My dad was still right, though. Andy is a lucky guy. Shirley and I had four sons. ☺ She had her four, and I had my four (three sons and a stepson). I like them both, good people, good friends.

In that same box, I found photographs of a beloved Swiss lady from Zurich. She spoke only German, Italian, and French (only?) while I spoke "soldier German" which could get me to a train station and a beer and a ham sandwich. Still, we wrote to one another a lot, and a fellow she knew was our translator. I came back to the States, and she didn't, and there are moments when I regret that. But there were just too many differences, language being foremost among them. I hoped to find her address, but I guess I threw away that old address book ages ago. Just wondering, is all.

The Christmas tree arrived today—artificial and boxed. I have not opened the box yet, because I would then have to set up the tree, and I'm not sure I have what it takes to do that. Maybe tomorrow morning. Tonight, I'll have the rest of those ribs, and I'll warm the darn things up in the microwave. Looking forward to Thanksgiving with son Haakon and his wife Lisa, and family. I am to bring a pumpkin pie. Don't worry, I won't make the pie. I found a place that specializes in pies. All I do is pick them up. Seems reasonable.

Fed the deer tonight, and wonder of wonders, a buck with a rack of horns showed up. That just never happens. He may be the fellow who visited in the spring with just a couple of knobs protruding from his head. Here in Lake Arrowhead, the males all tend to congregate at one end of the acreage, the females are the one that come here to 101 Corner Oak Court. That's fine, but this guy seemed to know me. He had some corn, looked over at me, and tossed his regal head as if to say "Thanks, Poppa Ace." Makes a guy feel good.

The cat wants her dinner, so I'd better quit. Just a mish-mash of stuff to write about anyhow. I hope you, dear reader, are having a good—even great—day. (Got to get that cat declawed!)

And Then This Englishman Shows Up At My Door

It's been quite a day. I've got all the 120 or thereabouts holiday greeting cards all set for mailing out after Thanksgiving sometime. They'll go out early, because there are folks out there who don't have a clue that I'm living in an old log cabin in North Georgia with a black cat named "Putih"—which, in Malaysian would get a roar of laughter because the word means "white". So that's a major project handled. Let the Post Office worry about it from here.

Got the tree up, too. You know the drill. Three sections, stick them together on a metal stand, try to find the plugs to get the lights on in each section, and hope for the best. Fluff out the branches so they somewhat resemble a pine tree's branches and feel that maybe I didn't spend enough on the darned thing. Branches fluffed, you add red streamers, a bunch of red balls, and a red bow for the top. Then you spend the entire rest of your day placing over 100 little straw goats, angels, bells, pine cones, and stuff—including one witch on a broomstick, one Mother Mary, and one old man, all made of straw. It just takes forever!

Next, it's the garlands. I spent a fortune on garlands this year. One fifteen-footer to fit on the mantle above the fireplace that doesn't work (the guys are coming with a whole new propane gas artificial log set in just a couple of days, and it will have a remote so I can turn it on and off from my chair without getting onto my knees). The other fifteen-footer I cut up to fit places where garlands should be. It didn't want to be cut up, but I happen to have a large electrician's cutter tool in my tool drawer. If that large electrician ever finds out who "borrowed" his cutter tool, I am in deep doo.

Had to go into Waleska to pick up mail that was deemed "too large for my box" by the U.S. Postal Service. The notice that I had such mail said, in the box for sender, "NAPA". Well, as a former Californian I thought of the Napa Valley and its wine production (some of it damaged by recent fires in northern California), and figured that my ex had sent me a case of wine for the holidays. But "NAPA" also is an auto parts store in Laramie, Wyoming. My high school buddy who owns that branch of NAPA Auto Parts had sent me the annual calendar—pretty girls standing by antique cars. The U.S. Postal Service had not wanted to fold the envelope and thereby do any damage to the pictures of the pretty girls, for which they and I were truly grateful.

And then, just as I was settling in for a bit of well-deserved (my own judgement) rest and a little glass of late afternoon red wine, there was a knock on the knocker on my door. It was an Englishman! I invited him in anyway, and despite the language barrier we had a fine conversation. I provided him with a Corona beer, he provided me with someone to talk to in an otherwise "talk to the cat" sort of day. He admired the work I had done, which was heartfelt I am certain. I am certain because he handed me an envelope inviting me to a Christmas Party at the home he shares with his Scottish wife. (Imagine that, for a moment.) ☺

And so it turned out to be a lovely day. I'll warm up an Atkins diet dinner tonight in the microwave and watch a bit of television. Busy, busy, busy! Living alone (well, except for the cat), retired, and still being mistaken for a person age 65 yesterday, by a guy who I told should never, under any circumstances, take a job in a circus where he would be guessing people's ages. Life is good!

A Joyous Time

The wonders of the holiday season are coming together here at the cabin in the North Georgia mountains. Cards are coming into my mailbox from all over the world, friends and family telling me of their lives and often including photos and invitations to visit or telling me of their hopes to visit my little cabin this coming year. Most mention their amusement at receiving my cartoon card of the cabin, myself, and the creatures who frequent this place, and are pleased by the letter telling them of my life and times in the year just past. I am so lucky, so happy, to have such wonderful people in my life. Joyful cards and letters.

Friends from sunny California came to spend a couple of days with me, leaving this morning. We had a grand time catching up on our goings and comings, dining on homemade "Southern" food, talking politics and even religion as our time together went racing by. They say they slept well, appreciative of the cool mountain night air. We all overslept a bit this morning, even the cat. It was such a joy to have that couple here for even a short visit. Joyful visitors, my friends.

After six months or so of planning and negotiating, the landscapers arrived and planted a large number of shrubs just day before yesterday. We've improved the look of the entrance to my driveway, created the beginnings of a leafy barrier between my place and the road out front, dressed up the yard itself with random plantings, and put in some beautiful flowering bushes near the steps that most folks think of as the main door to the place. The patio is bracketed with new plantings too, and there are ferns around the large stump of the huge old oak that had to be removed last summer. It's going to be gorgeous. The landscaper asked me, at one point, "Do you want smaller plants at less cost that will take several years to reach maturity, or larger plants?"

"I'm eighty-one years old," I replied, "so I probably better get the larger plants." We both laughed. Joyful laughter.

The plants are deer resistant, I'm told, but there are a couple members of the herd that visits me daily who find them irresistible. So, I've spent a good bit of time writing this, more than usual, because I've been chasing deer away between sentences. They particularly seem to enjoy ripping the newly planted ferns out of the ground. They don't eat them, actually. They just pull them up and leave them. It's going to be very cold tonight, and I can't get down on my knees to replant my new little ferns. I love the deer, but I've taken to feeding them their daily ration of corn out in the back, near where I park my car. They seem more than a bit confused when this old man rushes out into the cold to shake his cane at them. No more sense than God gave geese! But I love both my deer and my new ferns. Joyful confusion!

The artificial tree is covered with glowing lights. The fire is warm and wonderful in the fireplace, even though the logs aren't real. The cat is sleeping soundly in her bed. The wash is done, and the sheets and towels have been replaced. There is still enough low country shrimp boil left to provide a nice dinner tonight. The holiday decorations are up. Joyful evening is here.

The First Log Cabin I Owned ... And Christmas

The first log cabin was a cabin we designed and had built to our specifications, later adding a Master bedroom suite. It was located just four miles south of Blue Ridge, Georgia, and at 2,500 feet above sea level it was high on a ridge overlooking a fertile valley with a wonderful view of 4,000-foot mountains across the way. There were some flaws, sure, but I loved that place more than you can possibly imagine.

I loved it, in part, because each summer we would host a barbeque party with about 100 guests, many of them people we worked with all year. We'd supply tubs of barbequed pork and beef; they would be asked to bring the trimmings. With such a sizeable number of guests, we didn't have to tell anyone what to bring. It all worked out: baked bean dishes, potato salad, regular green salads, desserts of all kinds. Always a great afternoon for all in attendance.

I loved it, too, because of Christmas—and a visit we made to our cabin one special year, a couple of weeks before Christmas. We had driven up from the Atlanta area as we did almost every weekend and had dinner at a local Blue Ridge restaurant. We didn't stay at the cabin full time then—that came later. It had begun snowing a bit, an early December snowfall with thick, heavy flakes that stuck to everything except the roads. There was a couple seated near us in what can only be described as "the great room" where most customers were dining. A little boy, about six years old or so, was part of their party.

And then, in walked a fellow with a long white beard, and his lovely older wife with gray hair, and another couple, probably his son and wife, intent on finding a table for dinner. The little boy saw the group enter the room, led by the man with the long white beard. He leaped up, and before his folks could stop him, he began running up and down the room pointing and shouting, "THAT'S SANTA CLAUS! THERE HE IS! HE'S RIGHT HERE. THERE'S SANTA CLAUS!"

The old man looked over as the kid's parents were trying to catch him and "shush" him and motioned that they should let the boy come to him. The child's parents backed off, and the old man got down on his knees to the boy's level and began to talk with him. There was much head nodding, smiling, and hugging going on. Then the boy went back to his table, and the old man sat down with his family for dinner. And all the rest of us in the room grinned.

Turns out, the little boy was right! The old man with the long white beard donned a red costume every day this time of year and became "Santa" to countless children who sat on his lap in one of the large Atlanta department stores. He may have been the real Santa Clause after all.

We finished dinner smiling and drove up to our log home on the ridge. That night it snowed three feet deep, the power went out, and I had to make a wheelbarrow into a sled to haul more wood from the neighbor's place. Even with a four-wheel drive pickup truck, we couldn't get out of our driveway. We cooked over a camp stove, used a camp light to read by at night, and slept by the fireplace. And three days later, our sons drove up and we walked down to the bottom of the ridge to meet them and head home for badly needed showers. Thanks for being there, Santa.

Random Thoughts On December Twenty-Seventh

Woke up this morning (which is always nice to do at my age), and realized it was once again too cold up in the "Master Suite" to take my morning shower. It was yesterday, too. I'm beginning to gross *myself* out. I put on my heavy robe and came downstairs to turn on the gas space heater and the fireplace. Soon it will be "toasty" upstairs. Heat rises. Right now, the cat (who bathes all day long) won't even sit on my lap. This old cabin was built for folks who go to Florida in the winter, I think.

I've found that when Southern women like me, and feel sorry that I'm an old grandfatherly type who lives alone and is losing weight because I have no woman to cook for me, they bring me things to eat. Last night, for example, I had a slightly used lasagna dinner, garlic bread, and about a third of the largest piece of chocolate pie I had ever seen. I'll have the same dinner tonight. Waste not, want not. And cookies and candies, good grief! And one lady brought me a delicious meaty chili. Yesterday I had to go in for lab work ordered by my doctor, and I was afraid they would weigh me. They didn't. I was fully prepared to strip down to my shorts in an effort to lose a few of these holiday pounds I've put on. Didn't have to, and so the lab tech didn't start retching.

This old cat and I get along pretty darn well. Right now, she's lying in front of the gas space heater, soaking it in. If she's in an affectionate mood while sitting on my lap, she'll often reach out and touch my short beard, claws out to groom me, I suppose. She gives me "bumps" with her head on my chin, too. In return, I scratch her head and ears and back, where she can't reach. We have one of those symbiotic relationships, you might say. Ever since I hired landscapers to install shrubs and other plants in my yard, my deer have decided that they would like some salad before their daily shelled corn. I dash out, waving my arms in the air like a madman, and chase them off. The cat's on my side in this battle. Now, if deer enter the yard, she'll actually growl—like a dog—to let me know they're back. She also growls at neighbors walking their dogs in the street below the cabin. (Oh, and before you think too badly of me, I still do feed the deer corn—but on the other side of the cabin, down by the driveway where my car is parked).

I just love my Christmas tree, but I realize I'm going to have to take it down someday soon. It's covered with tiny goats (pagan symbolism), stars and angels (Christian symbolism—I'm an equal opportunity tree decorator), snowflakes, bells, and pine cones, all made out of straw by little old Norwegian ladies, I suppose. I doubt that many people enjoy getting back to "normal" after the holidays. Seems kind of dull then, when all those little lights are gone.

Today is the anniversary of my first wedding, to the mother of my sons. It was held in her hometown, Grinnell, Iowa. We traveled to Des Moines for our honeymoon. We probably are the only couple in history to have honeymooned in Des Moines, Iowa. We drank champagne out of blue and pink baby cups, because there were no glasses in our motel room, and none in the nearby grocery store, either. I never forget anniversaries. I do try to forget Des Moines. Enough said!

New Year's Resolutions For 2018

Well, it's that time of year again. Time to make a few New Year's Resolutions. I make them because I believe it's always good to have a plan, even if you don't follow it. Please note that I have not resolved anything about religion or politics (on paper). I do hope these resolutions will motivate others to get with the program. There's an even dozen. Maybe in 2019 I can resolve to convince my youngest son and the Executor of my estate (such as it is) that after cremation my ashes are to be sent to Blue Earth, Minnesota, for burial, not to Blue Ridge, Georgia. He's trying to save the estate some money, I suppose. But all that can wait, I think. These are my resolutions for 2018:

1. Take down the holiday decorations and tree sometime before Easter, which is Monday, April 2, 2018. (I might just leave the tree up. It's artificial and fills an empty corner of the cabin).

2. Contact Kaley Cuoco who plays Penny on "The Big Bang Theory" on television, to see if she would like to live with an old man in a log cabin in the North Georgia mountains. (Hey, nothing ventured, nothing gained).

3. Teach my cat to understand and speak English so that I don't have to feel so foolish telling her about my life and times, or don't have to listen to that "Meow" stuff every day not knowing what she's trying to say. (This whole idea may be a mistake, come to think of it).

4. Invest in an area winery, to reduce my costs at the grocery store. (I do a lot of cooking with wine. Sometimes I even put some on the food).

5. Get myself in shape. (Hey, round IS a shape!) (I did join one of those fitness clubs a few years ago, but then I found out you had to GO there).

6. Join one of those on-line dating clubs to find myself a hot chick around eighty years old or so to pal around with. (Most people my age are cold all the time, myself included. A hot chick might be just what the doctor ordered).

7. Change doctors. I talked to mine about the hot chick idea and couldn't get a prescription. (I might just quit going to doctors at all. The fewer I see, the better I seem to feel).

8. Train myself to sleep through the entire night without wetting

the bed. (Running that washing machine every day gets pretty expensive). (Uffda!)

9. Start wearing my hearing aids again. (Haven't worn them since I moved from California. I have no idea who these new neighbors of mine are, or what they're talking about).

10. Avoid remarriage. (Fool around a little, though). (Ha!! You're eighty-one, and you can't even dance. Forget it!)

11. Learn to dance with a cane. (I'd prefer to dance with a woman, but that's highly unlikely).

12. Travel to exotic places. (I may drive to Newnan, Georgia, next year to see the sights).

10. "Professionals" We Have Known And Loved

If you've ever owned an older home, or an older log cabin in particular, you'll recognize some of these characters who solve your problems. The cleaning lady is a "pro". So is the realtor who sold me this place. Electricity can be scary, so you call an electrician. Landscaping is a profession of sorts. The young fellow you call when mice, termites, carpenter bees, and other critters intent on living in your home is a professional. Even the guy from Sears who found the problem with my new dryer did so in a professional way. But the professionals I get the greatest kick out of are the two lovely "bag ladies" who appear regularly on my television set to sell me some stuff that will remove the bags under my eyes! (How did they know?)

Professionalism

Several times a week you probably hear the word "professional". It's always tied to something a person has done. "She did a very professional job with that paper." "He always behaves in a professional manner." And even, "Those people are true professionals." It's the word that describes knowing how to do something, doing it with expertise, doing it extremely well. It's not a word to be bandied about, used willy-nilly. It's a word that still means something, even in our cynical age.

The toilet paper roll in the guest bathroom downstairs in the cabin hangs directly above the vent for the heating and cooling system. As often as not I would walk in there and find about four feet of toilet paper flying in the breeze. I'd roll it back up on the roller, and in just a minute it would be flying again. "Stupid place to put a toilet paper roll hanger," I'd mumble to myself. Last week my cleaning lady came, apparently noticed the flying toilet paper (who wouldn't?) and turned the roll around on the hanger. Instead of rolling down the front, it now rolled down the back of the roller. Problem solved! "Professional." She knew what to do, did it, and fixed the problem!

A month or so ago I tried to charge the battery that powers my vacuum cleaner by plugging it into a wall socket in the kitchen. Immediately the entire row of outlets on that wall and the microwave stopped working. I went to the control panel and pulled a few switches, but nothing happened. Had to call an electrician. He arrived promptly (the mark of a "professional"), checked the control panel, and then walked over to one of the wall outlets and pushed a small button on the outlet. Everything worked!! He knew what to do, did it, and I had power for cooking again.

He said he hated to charge me anything for that, but my cabin is at no small distance from the real world, and so he had to be paid. He actually seemed embarrassed. I told him that he was being paid for what he knew, and that I had no problem with that. He was a "professional" in the real meaning of the word.

The realtor who sold me this cabin is a "professional." I had copied down his phone number from the for sale sign in the yard while visiting family in Georgia last December. Liked the look of the place from the outside. But I had to fly back to California without seeing the inside of the cabin or even meeting the realtor. When we spoke on the phone, he could tell I was really interested. It was a log home, old and a bit cranky as I am, with no yard to mow—just leaves. It was more than a bit unique, too, some would even say "odd"—sort of like me. But I hadn't a clue about the inside of the place and couldn't afford to fly back to Georgia to check it out. So, what did he do? He made a super film of the inside of the cabin, every nook and cranny, showing me all the things that I would have been looking at in person if I could have. He knew what to do, he did it with expertise, and he did it extremely well. I now own the cabin because that realtor was a true "professional."

Cleaning ladies, electricians, realtors, and anyone working to help another in almost any job you can name, can be a true "professional." Attitude, motivation, and knowledge are the only real keys to earning the accolade: "There goes a real professional", we just need more of them.

Power To The People

The power went out last evening at 5:30 p.m. The space heater on the dining room wall took over as did the fireplace, and soon it was a toasty seventy-seven degrees by my recliner. I turned off the space heater. It kept on snowing all night, and by morning we had nine or ten inches of the stuff in the yard. It was still beautiful, but the beauty was moderated somewhat by the fact that I was cold as the dickens and the cat didn't seem very warm either. I cranked up the space heater again. It got better.

The birds, though, were having a tough time of it. Snow had clogged the holes that let the seeds dribble out of their feeder, and the little water dish was frozen solid. They fluttered around, much to the joy of my indoor cat who wanted then to be an outdoor cat, until I brought them a baking dish full of seeds and a plastic glass filled with water. They came in droves. Made me feel I'd earned my keep as a member of the National Wildlife Association.

Thawing started before noon, and soon great globs of snow fell from the tall trees in my yard. The birds began playing "Dodge 'em" to avoid being globbered (clobbered, but with globs of snow), and it was a fun thing to watch for both the cat and me. They all made it, but their evasive actions would have put a U.S. Airforce jet fighter pilot to shame.

And then the huge old trees above the cabin began to drop their loads of snow. "Bam," "Kerplunk," "Ribbit ribbit ribbit" as they started avalanches on the snow gripping my steep roof. The cat was absolutely beside herself. "What is this new indignity I am forced to endure?" she meowed at me. I tried to explain. "It's just snow falling down the roof and onto the ground below." She wasn't having any of that explanation and charged off to one of the two guest bedrooms to seek protection elsewhere.

Actually, for the better part of the afternoon, it sounded as though Santa Claus and his eight tiny reindeer were landing, taking off, and landing again on my roof—as part of a training program for Rudolph, the red-nosed reindeer. I actually looked out, expecting to see a flash of that red suit as Santa got his charges into shape for a very long trip. (I saw nothing but snow). (Sorry, kids).

Several friends came by to chide me for having a Norwegian Christmas Party tomorrow and inviting Norwegian weather to come along. The fact that they got to my cabin at all, though, made me decide that the party was a "go," come hell or high snowfall. And so it will be, tomorrow. If need be, I'll cook the Swedish meatballs out on the grill. (Brushing the snow off the grill first, of course.)

And then at 4:00 p.m. the electric power came back on! Prayers were answered up and down Cherokee Drive and even at Corner Oak Court. Life began to return to normal, whatever that is.

It's Been One Of Those Better Days — The Electrician Came By

I wrote recently about some of life's small aggravations (see "IT'S BEEN ONE OF THOSE DAYS.)" My life here in the old cabin in the woods got a lot better today. The electrician came by.

Somehow, a couple of days ago, when trying to recharge the battery for my vacuum cleaner, I lost power in all the outlets along the kitchen counter and worse, the microwave. For two mornings, I've been making toast and coffee in the guest bathroom, hardly the place for any fancy cooking. The stove still worked, and so did the refrigerator, so I was not totally without resources. But I often get a "hankerin'" for some good old Swedish meatballs in sauce with noodles — Atkins Low Carb Swedish Meatballs, made in the microwave.

(As an aside: Atkins gives you nine meatballs and less noodles, while the other frozen food vendors give you only six meatballs and load you up on carbs. I know this stuff. I live alone).

Well, I was driving in to the grocery store early this morning (around 9:30 a.m., which is "early" for me since I am retired and not getting any younger) in order to beat the heat of the day, when the electrician called on my cell phone. I pulled into the Waleska Post Office parking lot, to talk with him (I drive more carefully since I got that damned cell phone and became a "senior citizen"). He'd be at the cabin in half an hour. I rushed back home, and he was right on time. I showed him the five double outlets and the microwave that weren't working. Then he walked over to one of the double outlets, pushed a button on the cover plate, and everything came on again. A blessed miracle if I ever saw one. (And no, I never before saw one). It put me in mind of a time up in Ashland, Wisconsin, on Lake Superior, where we lived in a 100-year old mansion that I bought for $17,000. The light in the bathroom went out. I got a ladder and put in a new bulb. Nothing! I grabbed another new bulb.

Nothing again! So, I phoned an electrician. He came out, put in another new bulb, and we had light in the bathroom! He charged me $50.00 for that experience. The guy this morning charged me $142.00!

He apologized. I was put into the odd position of consoling him by saying that what I really was paying for was his expertise. What he knew that I didn't. He left, feeling better, with my check.

I had, at one time, a small private practice. Charged $100.00 an hour, but I had expenses. Folks paid me for what I knew, and some of them got better just because they were paying me. So, don't drop out of school, kids, whatever that school you chose is teaching you. You need the expertise in order to make it in the world—as an electrician, a psychologist, or anything else.

So, it was a much better day, even though a costly one. And the bear didn't get my hummer juice last night (I brought it into the kitchen when it got dark); and I did get to the grocery store for my distilled water; and this morning I saw my little fawn and she was back with her mother. All's well that ends well. A much better day. And I'm having Atkins Swedish Meatballs tonight!!

Faced With A Fascinating (To Me) Dilemma

The half-acre of woodland that my log cabin sits on is almost totally wild. Not beautiful wild, but this time of year kind of ugly wild. Most of my visitors love the wild feel of this land of mine, particularly when deer come strolling through as though they owned the place (prior to 1975 when this cabin was built, they did), or when birds unusual to them (if my visitors have come from "a far piece") land on the feeder just a few yards away. But during the summer rains the leaves that cover the bare ground here sort of melt away, leaving ugly.

The lot is a corner lot. Sitting in my patio I look out onto Corner Oak

Court. No problem. My friends who live down in the "Court", and the occasional delivery truck, are the only vehicles on that road, and I love to wave at my friends. They wave back. But the road just in front of my half acre is a major thoroughfare here in Lake Arrowhead, and construction trucks pass by all day long. They sort of defeat the romantic notion that I am virtually alone in these woods, with the "ROAR" of their engines and the sight of their cabs rising above the ground I call mine.

And so, with those two issues as my rationale, I've been saving up to have a bit of landscaping done. Some pine straw where there are no fallen leaves, some shrubs to sort of dress up the entry to my driveway, more shrubs and evergreens near the little deck that people think is the front of the cabin (it's not, but I'm the only person around here who thinks it's not), and then a sight and sound block of shrubs and taller evergreens out by the road to reduce the noise and eliminate the sight of all those trucks rumbling past.

Got my plans approved by the Homeowner's Association. I'm quite possibly the only homeowner who has ever submitted a landscaping plan to the Board. Most just go ahead and plant. But I was a bureaucrat, and rules are rules you know. Then, yesterday, the owner of a highly recommended landscaping company came by to look at the plan, the property, and me. He shared his ideas, one of which was "Just go ahead and plant". Another was, "The shrubs approved by the Board won't grow here because there's too much shade." And then he said, "Would you want us to plant smaller shrubs and evergreens that will grow to maturity in about six to eight years, or would you prefer — at a higher cost, of course — that we plant some fairly mature plants that would have a better chance of making it through our warm summers?"

AND I THOUGHT: "Six or eight years?" "Greater expense for more mature plantings." And most importantly, "HOW LONG WILL I BE LIVING HERE?" And then, "HOW LONG WILL I BE LIVING?" In six or eight years, my sons will probably move me into an assisted living home and will hold an estate sale for all my stuff. "I'LL NEVER GET TO SEE THE PLANTS MATURE!" (Sometimes, in my darkest moods, I feel the same way about the great-grandchildren). I mean, when you're eighty-one, you begin to think like this. It's a real dilemma. Mature plants and more expense? Smaller plants and save some bucks for dating beautiful ladies?

"I'm eighty-one. Let's go with the larger plants," I told the landscaper. (Sorry, beautiful ladies).

This Is About "Austin", The Exterminator

Not too long after moving into 101 Corner Oak Court, I began to realize that I needed an exterminator. Oh, not the Chicago gangster type, since I enjoy being with all my neighbors down the road and have little interest in exterminating either of my two ex-wives, although the thought does occur at times. (Not really, I still love them both. They aren't that sure they still love me). I mean, I needed to get rid of bugs!

That was before I realized that I also needed to get rid of mice. I know they're cute little things and all that. It's just that mouse poop in strange places around the cabin, and holes eaten in such things as my hot pads (must have dribbled something from a casserole on the way to the table), a small hole in my sofa (it's no longer a "davenport" in this modern day and age) to get cotton batting or whatever manufacturers put in those things that mice think might make comfortable homes, and nibbles around the heavy-duty plastic containers I have for bird seed, can all be pretty aggravating.

There were already a host of green-topped things buried in the ground all around the cabin to ward off termites. If you live in a home constructed entirely of wood, you don't want termites anywhere near it. The containers had been placed in the ground before I bought the cabin and were doing an effective job. So, I called the company that put them in the ground, and I got Austin.

Austin arrived pretty close to the time he said he'd be here, a good sign. He was in a clean white uniform with his name on the shirt. Another good sign. He was young. (My God, isn't everybody these days?) He was eager to do well. He was personable. And he was as honest as the day is long. What's more, I liked him, and he liked me. So, he went to work on the mice. And the bugs.

My once-a-month cleaning lady came a couple of weeks later and found not a single sign of mice. The moths in the upstairs bedroom were gone, too. Then Austin spotted the holes made by carpenter bees all over the outside of my log home and gave me a price for eradicating them that I couldn't resist. Because of Austin, next year I won't be sitting in a pile of sawdust that used to be my cabin. He even wandered out (no extra charge) to wipe out nests of tent caterpillars that had infested a tree on my property line. Finally, he laid down a vapor barrier in my crawl space below the cabin that my son, who knows a thing or two about such stuff, said was a "great job!"

Austin is in his twenties, and married, and a little too old for me to adopt. Besides, I've got three great sons of my own already. But this young guy is going to go places in this competitive world of ours. Mark my words on that. He's got the attitude right and works hard to do the toughest jobs. His professional service as an exterminator has made my home here in the North Georgia woods a whole lot more livable. I'm impressed, in case you hadn't guessed.

But When A Tree Doesn't Meet Joyce Kilmer's Expectations…

Joyce Kilmer's famous poem, "Trees," spoke of a tree that, "…looks at

God all day and lifts its leafy arms to pray." There are a lot of wonderful oaks and pines in the yard at 101 Corner Oak Court, but there were two sixty-foot oaks, fourteen inches in diameter, right next to the patio, that didn't meet Joyce Kilmer's definition. Sadly, after many years of growing taller and more leafy, they had died. This summer all their leaves turned brown. One can only wonder why. Perhaps they just grew tired.

They did pose a danger to my cabin in the woods and had to come down. A young woman from the tree removal company phoned me last evening to tell me that the men who removes trees would be out early in the morning. "They like to arrive between 7:00 and 8:00 a.m." "Oh, really?" I said. "Then they are likely to see me in my nightshirt!" That didn't seem to faze her in the slightest. Perhaps she had seen a lot of men in their nightshirts, but I doubt it. Nightshirts are hard to find, while men's pajamas can be purchased almost anywhere (gas stations, grocery stores, medical clinics, and houses of worship being among the few exceptions).

Three men and a large truck pulling a tractor-like thing with blades like elephant tusks arrived at 7:30 a.m. Fortunately for all concerned, I had awakened at 6:50 a.m., went through my clean-up routine, and had just settled down to a cup of coffee when they showed up. They threw thin ropes at the end of a stone up into the tops of my trees, lowered the stone end to the ground, and attached much larger ropes to be pulled up, replacing the smaller ropes. Then, as if by magic, six or eight more men arrived. One, a large muscular guy, was the cutter. The others were rope pullers. The cutter cut, the pullers pulled, and down came first one tree, then the other. A third tree, much smaller, bent under the weight of the second tree to fall and snapped in two, so it was cut to the ground also.

Clean-up was brisk, to say the least. Everyone had a job and knew that job. The trees were cut into ten foot lengths and taken away by that tractor-like thing. Branches were placed in piles, and men hand-carried those piles to the waiting truck. Someone placed two large stones on the stumps of the downed trees—a ritual of some kind? Keeping tree vampires away? The lead guy came inside to collect the check. They were gone before 9:00 a.m.!

The cat hid under the bed for about half an hour after the tree removal men left. The birds seemed confused at first, but soon had found other trees to serve as their breakfast tables. The hummers were totally unfazed by the entire process. And me? I was amazed at how much closer those huge boulders in my yard seemed with the two trees gone and how bare the yard in front of my huge windows felt to me.

It was a job that had to be done, like it or not. I didn't like it. But it was done quickly, with precision, and an unexpected level of professionalism. The chain saws fell silent. It was over.

Doctorin'

Back when I was just a kid, maybe about ten years old or so, I got sick enough to have to stay in bed, even during the day. "Doc" Russ, our family doctor and also our neighbor just up the street, came by to check me out. He apparently decided that I needed a shot of some kind, administered in the "behind". I was told to roll over on my stomach. He prepared the needle. The lamp on my dresser cast a shadow on the opposite wall, the shadow of a huge needle! I watched it descend, fascination born of fear! I've never really felt all that comfortable around doctors or needles since.

Since then, I've had a long and sometimes strange relationship with doctors. Strange? Well, when I was in the Army of Occupation in Germany after the second World War, I came down with something or other, a cold or the flu, that required a visit to the doctor. The doctor happened to be a German. His prescription? Bed rest for three days, with a diet of red wine. I was probably the only soldier in military history who spent three days in bed in the barracks drinking red wine!

Out in California where I lived for six years, I was referred to an endocrinologist (say that out loud three times). Never having seen me before, he walked into the room where I was waiting to be examined and announced, "You have cancer!" That's what I would call a lousy bedside manner. I got up and left, told the referring physician that I would not see that fellow again, ever! And you know what? I did not have cancer. I did have a different endocrinologist, though.

Choosing doctors is nothing more than a game of chance. When I had my right knee replaced, I did a bit of investigating and then chose a surgeon named "John Henry". Why? Well, as the old song goes, "John Henry was a steel drivin' man, lord, lord! John Henry was a steel drivin' man." The new steel knee got infected, I wound up in ICU, and a surgeon from India whose name I never learned cleaned out the old knee and inserted a new one. I'll do more investigating next time.

What does all of this have to do with living alone as an elderly fellow in a log cabin in the North Georgia mountains? Well, anybody of my advanced age should have a primary care physician. I made an appointment with a doctor I'd seen in an advertisement. (Some of us just never learn). He proved to be a dud, stiff and formal, not eager to work with the geriatric set, and a person who failed to laugh at my little jokes. He did smile once, though. Fleetingly. I dropped him.

Today, my new primary care physician is a black female from Nigeria. I'm an old Norwegian. You would think we'd never hit it off. But this lady is an expert at listening. She smiles at my jokes. She's fascinated that I live in a log cabin. And she knows what she's doing. She explains things well. My only concern is that she may, at some time in the future, decide that I need a physical exam. I'm quite shy, as you may have noticed. I'd probably move back to California rather than put on one of those hospital gowns that are open in the back to have a physical exam done by this fine doctor from Nigeria! In fact, I'm sure of it.

So How You Doin'?

People everywhere, especially those who've seen me at least once before and feel they know me, always ask, "How you doin'?" My usual answer is, "Oh, I think I'll make it through the day." A very few will respond seriously with some comment meant to assure me that I will make it through the day. Most just look at my white hair and cane and grin. We'll see if they keep that grin when they are eighty-one and have arthritis in every bodily joint except one — and that one hasn't felt a darn thing for several years now! (OK, now you can grin).

Went to see a pain doctor yesterday afternoon. Actually, the correct title is "Non-operative Orthopedics and Sports Medicine Specialist". I find that kind of humorous. The closest I get to sports these days is flipping through the television stations to find a comedy show. Sometimes I watch the news, but that's pretty much of a comedy show these days too. I don't even have a pair of tennis shoes (I think they call them something else these days but the new name escapes me), or a jock strap, or even a shirt with a big number on the back. So "Sports Medicine" has nothing to do with me, nor I with it. I'm there for the "Non-operative Orthopedics" I guess. I do like the word "Non-operative". As surgeries go, I've been there and done that. Not pleasurable. I'm clearly there for the "Non-operative" stuff.

So, into the little room I'm sitting in, bounds — leaps and bounds — this kid! He's the doctor. I would have mistaken him for a grocery store carry-out boy if I'd seem him on the street. He says, "So, how you doin'?"

"I think I'll make it through the day," I responded. "Now, will you go get the real doctor?" He looked at my white hair and cane and grinned. We spent some time talking about arthritic knees, back, shoulders, and fingers. Then he said (he really did), "I have two needles. One is a little rusty, but it works really well. The other is brand new. Which would you like me to use for your cortisone shot in the knee?" I guess that's what "Non-operative" means. I opted for the new needle. He was back in a flash with a square needle so big it must have been used in veterinary medicine—on horses! I got my shot.

Generally, I'm doing pretty well. The arthritis is a pain in the everywhere, but otherwise you'd hardly believe I was eighty-one. I'm still extremely good looking, but I am having a little trouble with my glasses. They seem to be making everything look kind of fuzzy. I probably should see a "Non-operative Ophthalmologist", ya' think? Or get a better quality of glass cleaner. The doctors tell me I have a very low blood platelet count, and low red blood cells, so I am supplementing with some nice cabernet sauvignon wines. If I supplement enough, it even seems to be helping with the arthritis pain. I have a cyst in my brain that is pushing against my pituitary gland, which affects everything else in my system except that one bodily joint that I mentioned earlier. I am writing as fast as I can to get this book done before the cyst takes me over! But, ya' know, I think I'll make it through the day.

So, how you doin'?

A Nasty Sort Of Day For Man And Beast!

The day began well enough. Oh, it was cloudy, but cool and little if any humidity. Georgia in August is often covered over with air you could swim in. This was different. And if the outdoor temperature got above 75 degrees, I'd be surprised.

I'd had a tough time sleeping last night, though. When I was a kid, I fell out of a tree house that was under construction and broke my arm and shoulder. The doctor found the broken arm, but not the broken shoulder until my bitching about pain became unbearable for me, my family, and him. A bunch of doctors gathered 'round to decide that putting my arm in a sling was preferable to rebreaking the shoulder. No problem when I was a kid. But I'm no longer a kid.

At age 81, that damned shoulder hurts all the time, sort of like my knees do. And back does. So, while I like to sleep on my left side, I really can't. Sleepless nights are usually the result.

So, morning dawns. Up and at 'em! But somehow overnight I had developed a truly bad cold. No cold medicines in the cabin (what had I been thinking?). I staggered through my morning routines, fed the cat, fed the hummers, made a slice of thin rye toast for me, and plopped down in the recliner. "Plop!" I couldn't go into town for cold medications because the guy from Sears was coming "between 8:00 a.m. and 5:00 p.m." (nice big window) to fix my dryer, which had stopped working a full week ago. I prayed that he would arrive early. Most of my prayers go unanswered, probably because of what I pray for ☺, and my lack of faith in any deity but Odin. But, unbelievably, the fixer guy showed up a 10:00 a.m.! I might make it with the one clean set of underwear I had left, after all. (Hope springs eternal. I may have problems with faith, but I'm a sucker for hope).

He started to work on the dryer. I went to sit in my recliner. About twenty minutes later he came out of the laundry room and announced, "I have some very bad news for you." I thought, "What the hell? He's not a doctor!" He then said, "I took a picture of it". Sure enough, he had.

Apparently, back the week before, when I turned on the dryer to dry my sheets and towels, I had mercilessly killed one of the chipmunks!! Got in through the vent pipe, I guess. That's why I hadn't seen but one of them for the past week! In a week's time, bad things start to happen to the bodies of chipmunks killed by dryers. I don't know if it was the guy chipmunk or the girl chipmunk, we'd need an autopsy to be sure. The Sears dryer fixer guy and I were unable to perform that task. We closed the dryer back up, since the interior workings had been pretty much destroyed. He didn't charge me for the house call.

I drove into town to Sears, bought a new dryer for $500 and change, went to the drugstore for my cold medications and a back brace, and drove home. Sears will deliver the new dryer tomorrow. They will take away the old dryer, chipmunk and all. I am so very sorry. It was a nasty day for man (me) and beast (chipmunk). Not sure I'll tell the guys who are coming to take away the old dryer.

The Bag Ladies

You've certainly seen them. Two rather attractive blonde women, maybe in their forties, who come into your home via your television set to tell you about bags under the eyes. The lady with the long blonde hair plays the part of a reporter, fascinated by a newly discovered substance that removes those bags under the eyes. The other lady, with short blonde hair and a sort of robe-like outfit, plays the part of an expert in the scientific field of bag removal. She's actually, "So excited!" Why? Because in just five minutes using this newly discovered substance you can remove the bags under your eyes. She tried it on her father (an old guy, apparently, unable to defend himself) one day recently and in just five minutes the bags under his eyes were gone! When questioned about the composition of the substance that you rub under your eyes, and the length of time the bags remain gone, she seemed a bit vague.

A male actor with huge bags under his eyes, who looks a bit like an aging gangster of the Capone era, then appears and begins rubbing whatever it is under his right eye. As the two ladies talk, the camera watches the bag under his right eye disappear. The bag under his left eye also seems to shrink a bit, but that may only be due to the photographer's art.

There's another lady, much older, who comes on television and assures you that "I'm not going to lie!" She says the stuff REALLY WORKS.

What's more, it works on other places in need of a little tightening, too. Wrinkles disappear. Heaven only knows what else can be tightened! I don't want to think about it. She is followed by before and after photos of some ladies who weren't very pretty in the "Before" shot and didn't show much improvement in the "After" shot either.

All you need is some of this stuff made out of shale rock, bags under your eyes, and a clean, dry face. Oh, and five minutes of down time.

Before I'd met these ladies and that poor guy with huge bags under his eyes, I'd never given bags under my eyes much thought. But this morning, as I cleaned and dried my face, I couldn't help but notice that there were, in fact, bags under my eyes. They weren't the big galumphing bags like those you have to check in when traveling by air, but more like small carry-on bags. Still, I will probably break down and buy some of that shale rock stuff next time the two ladies appear on my television set. I really need all the help I can get. I'm single, you know.

And after all, if you can't trust two rather attractive blondes, who can you trust?

11. "Getting On In Years" Isn't For Sissies

For a few people, the "Golden Years" are just that: golden. For most of us though, aging is not an easy thing (but it does beat the alternative). Time moves by ever more quickly it seems, and things happen to you that just wouldn't have happened twenty years earlier—even, maybe, ten. When you're sick, you're *really* sick. When you have pain in the joints, you have *real* pain. Forgetfulness, often thought of negatively, can actually become a friend. And sometimes you meet people (mostly medical people) who you wouldn't have come to know as a young "whipper-snapper". And you get lots of mail—some of it about cremation. At least I do.

Thinking About Growing Older

Realized this afternoon, after sweeping the patio in the heat of the day, that I'm getting older. Some years ago, I would have swept the patio, then the driveway, then cut weeds back, and then maybe spread some pine straw. Nothing like a hot summer afternoon and a myriad of outdoor chores crying to be done to make a guy feel his age. Days like this make me realize that I'm never going to be good at golf, particularly since I would have to carry a golf club *and* my cane.

The lady I hired to help with the cleaning of this old log home once a month will be coming tomorrow morning. I've noticed some dirt in a corner of the guest bathroom for a couple of weeks now, but I can't get down on my knees to clean it up. Last time I tried that I couldn't walk for two days. Glad I'm not Episcopal. All that kneeling. Uffda. I've decided I'm going to leave baggies of snacks all over the cabin, just in case I fall down. When I was a kid, I always wanted to be older, but this stuff is not what I expected!

And have you noticed that everybody whispers? Of course, now that I'm single, I don't wear my hearing aids anymore. Nobody to nag me. But the neighbors are starting to complain that my television set is too loud, and my closest neighbor is a half mile away. And I do use more four-letter words than I did when I was younger. Words like "what?"

There are well-meaning people who try to tell me that age is all in the mind. They say, "Think old and you'll *be* old!" I say, "At my age, think young and you'll be delusional." I've still got a functioning brain I think, but I must admit that I do forget names a lot. But that's alright. I have friends who have forgotten that they ever knew me. And we went to high school together. I hate it when I see an older person and then realize we went to high school together.

When I went into the Army at age eighteen, I weighed 120 pounds, dripping wet. Now I'm twice the man I was when I went into the Army, almost exactly. I try to lose weight, but my metabolism works against me. I've got three sizes of clothes in the walk-in closet here in the cabin, two of which I will undoubtedly never wear again. I keep them around for nostalgia's sake. But I'm no good at clothes shopping. Fifty years ago, I bought the last "Nehru Jacket" ever sold in the United States. Still have it. Bought a light blue "Leisure Suit" (remember them?) thirty years ago. I looked like an Easter egg. Still have it.

But aging is not such a bad thing if you remember that age gets better with wine. And friendships grow stronger because we are aware of the swift passage of time. And you still know the words to all the old songs, and there are musicians who still play those songs. I have a good friend who is one. And I sing along. And there are grandchildren and even great-grandchildren, and how did my kids manage to have such wonderful children? Gladdens the heart. Aging happens, and while life was a lot easier when everything worked with just an "ON" and "OFF" switch, I have learned to operate my new cell phone (mostly). They tell me the darn thing can even take pictures. Ha! Don't try to fool an old man! I didn't just get off the boat, y'know!

Thinking About Time

There is an ancient proverb that tells us "Tide and time wait for no man". Or woman, I might add. And for those of us in our later years, it seems that time speeds up. At least that's how it appears to me.

Every morning my big black cat and I have a little ritual. I come down the stairs and she's waiting there. We head for the kitchen where I brew my morning cup of coffee and fill her bowls with fresh food and water. Then we head to the living room and after carefully setting the coffee cup down I fall into my recliner and lean back a bit. She looks up at me, I look down at her, and then she leaps into my rather ample lap as I shout, "Good morning, Putih!" She tromps on my chest a bit to assure herself that it's OK to be there, and settles down, purring. As I pat her head and scratch behind her ears, she tries to get the shiny pen out of my pocket or attacks one of my shirt buttons. We play this little ritualistic game every single morning.

This morning, for some reason or no reason at all, I began to think about time. It seemed that no time at all had passed between going through this "Good morning, Putih" thing today, and doing the very same thing yesterday, and the days before that. I know that I went to the dentist yesterday, picked up my clothes at the cleaners, and did all sorts of other activities both important and frivolous. I know that intellectually, but there still is a sense that no time had gone by since my last visit to the cleaners, and certainly since yesterday's greeting of the cat.

Perhaps it's my age. Friends who are about my age (mostly high school friends since I "run" with a much younger crowd in their fifties and sixties here in North Georgia) tell me that time zips past for them, too. It picks up a real "head of steam" (old railroad jargon) when you're in your eighties. Oh, and about those younger friends: they love being seen with me since, by comparison, I make them look so much younger. At least I think that's their reasoning.

Perhaps it's this holiday season with activities galore: decorating the cabin, wrapping gifts for family, partying with friends, getting all those greeting cards ready to send, planning a party, and on and on. Time moves quickly when you need to use every possible minute!

Maybe it's sleep patterns. I'm going to bed pretty early these days, and while I used to have to get up three or four times a night to use the facilities, I'm now up only once before that cat starts telling me it's time for breakfast. It just doesn't seem that I took the time to actually sleep those eight or nine hours. Whatever the cause, I am fully convinced that time waits for no man. I can only imagine that the tides don't wait around either.

You'd think, wouldn't you, that an old retired guy living alone in the woods would have all the time in the world. He'd probably even be bored to tears, poor old fella. But time waits for no man, and certainly not for this guy. I may just pour myself a small glass of red wine late this afternoon and steal a bit of that fast-moving time just to relax a bit. It's time I did.

Some Things That Happen... As You Grow Older

Just ruminating a bit this morning, trying to outwait the icy cold outside (hasn't been above freezing on Corner Oak Court for days) before heading into town for more apple-flavored deer corn. Got to thinking about things that happen more frequently as age creeps up on us. Here are three of the many weird things that seem to be happening to me:

Dropping Stuff: This morning I dropped some medications on the bathroom floor and had to bend down to retrieve them. I haven't been able to bend over and touch my toes since my Army days, and here I was, bending over to pick up pills. I'm far more spry now than I've been in quite a while. Getting my exercise the hard way, while swearing like a sailor. Sometimes it's my pen, or a sheet of paper vital to my future, or my Swiss army knife. I move those feet quickly when I drop that rascal, let me tell you. Once it was even *The American Heritage Dictionary*. Between dropping things and climbing those thirteen stairs to my little art studio and bedroom several times a day, I'm getting a lot of exercise. Guess it's nature's way of keeping us old-timer's fit!

Remembering Stuff: So, I'm going along, minding my own business, and suddenly a song from the 1950's will begin to play in my head. Or I'll recall how to order a filet steak with egg in German, but I'm in the bathroom shaving. Or a nonsense rhyme from third grade pops up:

"Oh, yes, ah is knotty pine, I'se just a wild columbine
Growin' midst the woodland vine.
Purple mountains 'round mah brow, purty as a yeller cow." (Pogo)

No apparent deep-seated reason for it that I can find, remembering stuff just seems to happen. After eighty-one years on this Earth, there's a lot of stuff in this old brain to remember, I can tell you. And to (hopefully) forget.

Trying Not to Do Dumb Stuff: At age ninety-five, my sainted mother would get up on a chair to put foil over the smoke detector in her little apartment whenever she was going to cook. Uffda! I walk down the stairs hanging on to the railings for dear life and walk upstairs the same way. And I move s…l…o…w. Moving around quickly as you grow older can be hazardous to your health. So, can chasing after fast women. My crazy brother-in-law sent me an e-mail address for an organization that wants to hook me up with Norwegian women. Really! Aside from the national anthem and a prayer, I don't even speak the language. I am trying not to follow up on that e-mail address. I try not to do dumb stuff. If I do too much dumb stuff, my sons will put me away. I don't want to be put away. I'm enjoying life in my log cabin in the woods, taking it slow and easy. My cat has been teaching me, by example, to take things slow and easy. She sure does…

More Stuff That Happens When You're Aging

A couple of weeks ago I got to thinking about stuff that happens when you're getting on in years, like dropping stuff, remembering strange stuff, and even trying not to do dumb stuff. Wrote about those thoughts. As if that weren't enough, here's more:

Sleeping Stuff: An old friend (of which I have many, all old) sent me a note telling me that she's sleeping a lot more now than ever before in her life, asking if that's "normal". "Why heavens yes, sweet thang," I told her. "I do it myself, so it must be normal." I haven't seen the 11:00 p.m. news for at least a year now. Get in my full ten hours of sleep a night, and sneak in one or two more with the cat on my lap in the recliner some days. Sleep helps you avoid a bunch of other stuff that you'd rather not do. It's nature's way of protecting the elderly from stuff.

Cooking Stuff: Remember the old joke about how a bunch of guys hired a prostitute to proposition an old friend (of which I have many, all old). She knocked on his door, and said, "I'm here to give you some super sex!" He replied, "If it's all the same to you, my dear, I'll just take the soup." Well, by golly, when you get up there in years that old joke isn't funny anymore. Most of us would take the soup. Used to be that I would whip up some pretty fancy dinners, with salads and sides. Now "fancy" is Marie Callender's frozen Honey Glazed Chicken Dinner with green beans. But I'll happily settle for a bowl of Campbell's Chunky Chicken Noodle Soup, a few crackers, and a glass of wine to wash down my pills.

Medical Stuff: Pills? Glory be! I take a dozen (count 'em) with breakfast (a slice of toast with an egg, maybe, if I'm feeling really frisky), and another nine with dinner (thank you, Marie). Some of them are over-the-counter stuff like Vitamin D, Calcium, ABC Senior Multi-Vitamin with Lycopene (what the heck is Lycopene?), and Glucosamine/Chrondritin for my knees. But there are quite a few with fancy doctor-made-up names like Amoxicillin for my chronic infections or Omerprazole for heaven only knows what! Well, heaven, pharmacists, and doctors, actually. Those made-up names are designed to keep the mystery in doctoring, and to separate the patient from the provider. And they give the doctor a chuckle when we patients try to pronounce them.

Falling Down Stuff: Five of my good friends have broken bones by falling in the past year. Most were just walking along, minding their own

189

business, when suddenly their "business" hit the ground. One even took a flying leap down a whole flight of stairs. Not good! I try to send cards. So far, I've not fallen (knock on wood). (Living in a log cabin makes that knock on wood stuff easy). It takes me half of the morning to get down those thirteen steps from my bedroom to my recliner. I'm ultra-careful. Never go anywhere in a rush! My canes help a lot. I really believe that the government should issue a cane to everyone when they reach age seventy. I've been thinking about putting in a fireman's pole so that I can just slide downstairs in the morning. Imagine the time that would save for sleeping in my recliner! But climbing that pole to get upstairs every evening might be problematic. It would sure build upper arm strength, though.

Let all of this be a lesson to you.

Sicker Than A Dog!

Alright, you dog lovers! I apologize. But it's just a phrase in common usage, not an indictment of all dogs. All it's saying is that I've been really sick. Too sick to:

- Get the mail for three days now. (Could be bad. These days, danger no longer falls out of trees, it falls out of envelopes!);
- Go into town, get corn for the deer, feed the deer. (They look reproachfully at me with those big brown eyes and it's almost more than I can deal with. I've dated brown-eyed ladies! Same thing);
- Pick up my clothes at the cleaners. (I'm beginning to look like an old man who lives in a log cabin in the woods).

Started with a slight headache and a fever around 6:00 p.m. on Wednesday. Then I got the shivers and cranked up the space heater built into the dining room wall. Still had the shivers. Also had to get into the bathroom to pee, over and over, every half hour. I went to bed at 8:00 and found that I had to get up every half an hour to hit the bathroom again, and again, and again! *All night long*! I do believe that I have a bladder infection. I've had them before, in California, and my ex-wife would rush me to the hospital because she wouldn't be able to sleep well with me getting up every half an hour *all night long*. Enlightened self-interest, she'd call it.

Parenthetically, I find it fascinating that the cat has now taken a great interest in bathrooms. If she were human, I'd call it a fixation. If, in my rush to get squared away in the bathroom, I forget to shut the door, there she is — climbing into the bathtub, then across the back of the toilet, and into the sink where she nuzzles the faucet. It's pretty disconcerting to be seated on the "throne" (I am now too old to pee standing up) and have a cat asking, "Whatcha doin', dad? Whatcha doin?" Uffda, as my sainted Norwegian mother would have said.

Thursday night I somehow knocked my flashlight off the side table by my bed. A few minutes later I dropped the cell phone/camera thing that tells time down between the bed and the table. Without the flashlight, I couldn't find the phone. Life can be maddening sometimes.

I'm feeling some better today, Saturday, and my trips to the bathroom are about an hour and a half apart now. But I still don't dare to drive into town. I thought maybe if I took a large paper cup I could make it there and back, but then I saw this little girl in my mind, asking her mother, "Mommy, what is that old man doing in that car?" And her mother saying, "Don't look!! I'll call the police. They know all about what old men do in cars!" Uffda, as my sainted Norwegian mother would have said. But at least she would have driven to town to buy deer corn.

I've been living on a liquid diet. Cranberry juice with my pills, Campbell's Chunky Chicken Noodle soup for my dinner. A friend suggested I should drink beer to push the infection out of my system. Now I'm out of beer. Guess now that I absolutely must get that paper cup and head to town, for sure. Priorities are priorities, after all. A man has got to have some beer! And that little girl shouldn't be anywhere near a store that sells beer.

Pain

I'd really make a lousy spy. If I were captured and taken to a little room to have my fingernails pulled out one by one, I'd tell them everything I knew. I have a very low pain threshold. The last few days have been pretty painful. While I hate to admit that I've been feeling a lot of pain ("macho" me) it's a significant part of life in this old cabin just now so it needs to be addressed.

A lot of people experience pain daily, often much worse than mine, so I am not complaining. Just explaining. The weather is going to change, probably tomorrow, and highs for the day will drop ten or more degrees. I look forward to fall (leaves are starting to change color and drop onto my driveway as I write), but transitions bring me pain. On the plus side, I can predict the weather as well as they do in those television newscasts. On the negative side, my mobility is hampered by the arthritis in my knees and lower back. I have to force myself to be an active participant in the world. Even taking the trash out to the trash can becomes a chore. "How long can I put this off?" I ask myself. My trash bag burps and says, "Hey man, not much longer. I'm full!"

There's arthritis in my left shoulder from a childhood accident, making sleep difficult some nights. It's also in my fingers and hands. Yesterday I wrote checks (yes, I'm an old-fashioned guy), and then addressed holiday greeting cards (yes, I am really ahead of the curve this year), and my handwriting was absolutely atrocious! My signature on those checks looked like the scribbling of a child, and the cards may never get to their intended recipients. As my sainted mother would have said, "Uffda!" Not complaining, just explaining.

A friend called to remind me of an outdoor event down by the lake last night and asked if I was planning to attend. I made up some stupid excuse about having my dinner cooking, because I just didn't want to tell him that I was in so much pain I could hardly move ("macho" me, again) much less get to a party at the lake. I do know that's ridiculous. I tried to avoid discussing pain during the last year or two of my marriage. For several years I would walk a pretty good distance every day, twirling my cane and feeling pretty good, but then the pain became too great to walk much. I even found standing difficult for any length of time. I had to sit down a lot, not because I was exhausted but because I was in such pain. We visited Norway with friends, and there were a couple of hikes I just couldn't make myself take with them. Physical pain can have some very negative effects on sharing life's little excursions with others. On the big excursions, too.

A couple of years ago my physician prescribed oxycodone for my pain, which was not nearly as severe then as it is now — twenty tablets. I have a dozen left. I should have discarded them months ago. I'm almost afraid to take them. The prescription says I can take two a day. Hah! I'd be a quivering mass of protoplasm if I did that! Don't want to get hooked on that stuff. I guess I prefer the pain. At least I know who I am. Emotional pain is not as great a problem for me as it can be for some people. Physical pain though is another matter entirely. Again, in view of the pain that others experience each and every day, I am not complaining. I'm just explaining. Tomorrow my pain may very well be almost gone. I hope that theirs will be almost gone, too. Hope might make a difference.

Forgetfulness

How in the world do I seem to have overcome diabetes? The answer, in a word, is "forgetfulness".

On the ten foot long mantle above my rustic stone fireplace in the living room of this quirky old log cabin that I have come to call "home", there are about fifty artifacts representing moments in my long life. They jog the memory every time I glance up at them. For example, there is the colorful and flowery porcelain plate that once belonged to Shirley Temple. It's mine because my mom was a good friend of Tippi Hedrin's mother. Tippi, who had a starring role in Alfred Hitchcock's film "The Birds", was a good friend of Shirley Temple. The plate followed that chain all the way down to me.

Or, for example, there is an ancient ceramic beer mug, gray with dark blue lettering "HB", the container for my very first German beer, which I drank at the famous Hofbrau House in Munich on the way to my Army barracks in the Alps and a new life with the armed forces occupying Germany after World War II. There's a model of my first car, a 1930 Ford coupe convertible with a rumble seat, and my high school dream car, a 1940 Ford coupe with teardrop fender skirts. There are memories galore above my fireplace, and I've forgotten none of them—yet! Good exercise for the mind.

But just this morning I cleaned up, dressed, and hobbled down the thirteen stairs from my bedroom suite (it even has a small balcony over-looking the oak forest out back) to the kitchen, and then realized I'd forgotten to bring my cell phone, eyeglasses, and wrist watch with me. Back up those thirteen stairs—clomp, clomp, clomp—gather those daily essentials, and then—clomp, clomp, clomp—back down those thirteen stairs.

Breakfast, then—clomp, clomp, clomp—back up the stairs with bird seed (I forgot to bring it upstairs with me last night), for those of my feathered friends who prefer to dine from the feeder on my balcony. And—clomp, clomp, clomp—back down again. Then it's time to drive six miles to metropolitan Waleska, population 300, to mail checks for all the monthly bills, and—oops! Forgot my shoes. Where? Upstairs! Clomp, clomp, clomp—put on the shoes—clomp, clomp, clomp—back down the stairs. Good grief. I left my cane up there! Clomp, clomp, clomp—up and down one more time.

Thirteen stairs up, thirteen stairs down. And so it goes. Some folks say that weight loss and a daily exercise regimen can, over time, beat diabetes. In my case though, the most basic reason for successfully dealing with diabetes is forgetfulness. Agreed?

Panic Attack

Ever had a panic attack? Not a whole lot of fun. Until last night I had never experienced one, but in my work as a psychologist with college students, I often encountered the darned things. Usually they could be linked to worry about a test, low grades, the Vietnam War (those days). One young lady had panic attacks whenever she walked past a certain church, because she'd once had to leave in the middle of a sermon and was seated near the front—so everybody was looking at her as she walked out. Often the "cure" was simple enough: "Visualize a chest of drawers. Open one of those drawers. Now, imagine yourself putting this fear of yours into that drawer. Now slam it shut!" But that only worked if you knew the cause.

Sometimes the cause of panic attacks is not very clear at all. We may wake up from a dream, heart beating faster than usual, unable to breathe, feeling weakness and an unreasonable fear . . . of what? Those can be more difficult to deal with. And the drawer won't stay shut!

Yesterday was an odd sort of day for the old guy living in the cabin.

It began with an appointment with a new primary care physician. The nurse did the blood pressure thing, and mine was pretty high. No reason that I could see. The doctor informed me that I had an enlarged prostate, which I either had never known or had forgotten about (motivated forgetting is a great little defense mechanism). A change in medication was called for. My white blood cell count was extremely low, low enough to cause a look of real anxiety on the doctor's face. Another change in medication. My endocrinologist wants me to start taking a testosterone-like drug costing $635.76 monthly, which is utterly insane. Problem is that the insurance companies must think that I'm trying to improve my sex life. The joke's on them. I have no sex life. I'm 81 years old! So, we are looking into alternatives to build up my flagging energy level. I didn't know it was flagging until the doctors told me. I thought a mid-afternoon nap in my chair was normal for my age. (Still think so, and still grab a few winks from 2:00 to 3:00 p.m. most days.)

Then I had a call from the head of "Property Management" here at Lake Arrowhead. I had submitted a drawing and write-up of some relatively minor plantings I wanted to do to improve the look of the place. "The Homeowner's Association Board won't approve these plantings because the plants you have selected are not native to this area," he said. I said, "But they are deer resistant." He said, "Well, the Board will probably make some recommendations to you." "Fine," I said. "I bow to the superior judgement of the Homeowner's Association Board. Just get me an approval, OK?" "OK." (A neighbor said, "Just plant what you please, and don't tell.")

Tonight I am putting a nurse, two physicians, a blood pressure cuff, my prostate, my white blood cells, my sex life, testosterone, my energy level, the head of "Property Management", the Homeowner's Association Board members (all of them), and a bunch of trees and shrubs into an imaginary drawer—a great big imaginary drawer. And then I am nailing it shut! I've got to get some sleep! Nothing like some good sleep to improve a guy's energy level. (I will feed the folks in the drawer twice a day and will provide them with water and maybe some red wine, if you were worried about them. I'm not cruel, after all. Just an old tired psychologist.)

A Visit To An Urgent Care Facility

It was a really aggressive, self-diagnosed, and damned annoying urinary tract infection. I'd had it for several days, but that included several nights when I was trotting off to the bathroom almost every half hour. Hard to get any REM sleep when you're awake every half hour, although I did have some dreams. In one, I was to give a speech in a hotel in Atlanta, but had trouble finding the hotel, and when I did find it I had even more trouble finding the room I was to speak in. In fact, I woke up to head for the toilet before I ever did find that room. A commentary on my infection I suppose: I was unable to find a way to deal with it effectively. (Thanks, Freud, but it had nothing to do with sex, and I figured it out myself.)

So, I called youngest son Haakon in the morning and we agreed that he would drive by and get me at about 1:30 p.m. I got stuff together for a hospital stay, since I'd had these things before, and they always resulted in a hospital stay. Fed and watered the cat, too. My son arrived, and we were off to the Urgent Care facility, not a hospital emergency room, to minimize the risk of hospitalization and red Jello instead of red wine for a few days. (It worked).

Got there at about 2:15 p.m., handed over my driver's license (proving once again that I was who I said I was) and my insurance cards, and in return got a five-page document to fill out. Questions so weird and personal that I was forced to reflect about my entire life to respond to most of them. I was assured that the facility people wouldn't share them with the media. Still, I lied a few times. When I turned in the forms, I was assured that I'd be seen by a competent professional within the next hour and a half. In the meantime, my son and I sat in a waiting room filled to the rafters with folk of all ages suffering from the flu. A coughing, wheezing, sneezing mob, that didn't appear to need to use the men's restroom.

A young lady showed me where the restroom was located. I mentioned to her that I thought I had a urinary tract infection. As I was opening the door, she hollered, "WAIT!" If you've ever experienced the urgency that a urinary tract infection brings with it, you'll realize just how silly that was. She came running with a little bottle and asked for my name because it was her job to write my name on that little bottle. When I told her my full name, she looked kind of sad, and asked me to spell just my last name as she wrote it. I suppose I was the only "Hagebak" who had to pee in a bottle there on that day, so the last name would be enough. I barely made it. Two hours later, my son and I were ushered into a small room in the back. A pretty blond nurse arrived and took my "vitals". She was followed by a pretty blond Physician's Assistant, who told me that my diagnostic skills were excellent. I did, in fact, have a severe urinary tract infection. She was followed by the pretty blond nurse, who gave me a shot of something in my left buttock. She also informed me that fourteen pills would be waiting for me at my downtown pharmacy.

As my son and I were leaving in the late afternoon, he turned to me and said, "Well, dad, we lucked out. Did ya' see that doctor? He was sure nothing to look at!" So, I went back and thanked the two young blond health care providers, just to be sure I'd made a good impression. You never know. One or both of them might feel that eighty-one-year-old psychologists who live in log cabins in the woods are quite interesting. Or maybe their grandmothers? I'll wait and see.

It's Been Raining On My Parade!

Even at the exalted age of eighty-one, when realistic plans for handling serious illness should clearly have been made, bad stuff pounces on you when you're not quite ready for it. So it was that late in January I arose from my bed to rush off to the bathroom, but instead fell to my knees before realizing that the recurring infection in my artificial knee had "recurred" again. Over a period of several hours I crawled on my elbows to the phone and dialed "911". It took our team of emergency folks here in Lake Arrowhead only minutes to get to my old log cabin and me—once I remembered the code to the door.

Off we went to the brand-new hospital, first the emergency room where I think I was heavily dosed with pain killers, then to a wonderful room with a view and a twenty-two year-old nurse who I immediately fell in love with. Age differences mean little when you're in love, but pain killing drugs can make damned fools of us all. Over the next week, she and I worked through the issues involved, and she decided to go ahead with the wedding scheduled next November for herself and the soldier she loved. The pain killers wore off, and her decision began to make sense. After all, I was married seventeen years the first time, forty the second time, and I'm exhausted!

The cat, "Putih", found a temporary home with some fine people who treated her well, and son Haakon (armed with a previously signed document granting him entirely too much authority over my life) wrote my checks, managed my medications, and moved my clothes and toiletries downstairs to one of the guest bedrooms where my great-great grandfather stares at me from his portrait each night as I crawl into bed. "If I find any evidence that you've been upstairs, I'll…" Thankfully, my son never finished that sentence. I have not been upstairs. He built a barrier!

After the hospital, I did three weeks in a rehabilitation center. The room was very nice, with a view that let me watch the comings and goings of families visiting their versions of me. My family visited me, too. The nurses were great—attentive, pleasant, patient. The physical therapists were also attentive, though I would have preferred that they had forgotten about me. The food, though, was absolutely terrible! I ate what bits of it I thought might be edible and lost another fifteen pounds. "This is NOT Southern cooking," the nurses would tell me. "I know, I know!"

Now I'm home in my log cabin with a brand-new bright red walker that has a seat built in. There's also a home health aide five hours a day, a nurse who comes in regularly to check my "vital signs", an occupational therapist who is amazed that I can actually dress myself each morning, and a physical therapist intent—I believe—on doing me great bodily harm. But neighborhood guys stop in to visit almost every day, and their ladies often bring me treats to brighten my spirits. The cat comes home this week, maybe Thursday. And my family loves me.

So, the rain that has been falling on my parade seems to be moving away, and I am gradually getting better. Spring is on its way to these North Georgia mountains!

A Special Word For The "Neptune Society"

It's the day after Thanksgiving. For many here in Lake Arrowhead, Christmas is just around the corner—or some other equally grand holiday. These weeks together form a time of joy, family togetherness, great fun with grandkids, and even greater fun just being alive to enjoy all of this. And then, in today's mail, I got a nice little letter from the Neptune Society telling me that "Time stands still for no one". Uffda!

The Neptune Society folks have asked me to take the time now to make an affordable, sensible choice. I guess I'd choose another helping of turkey and dressing with a wee bit of that gravy and another slice of that bourbon pecan pie, thank you. But no, I'm supposed to take the time to make my "Cremation Prearrangements". They tell me that I am the best person to deal with this responsibility now, while it can be handled without stress or unnecessary expense."

Without stress? Good grief! I've got to get the tree up and decorated, plan a menu or two, make sure the sheets on the beds are clean and fresh, get out the greeting cards to half the population of Earth, worry about gifts ordered that haven't come yet, and hit the Post Office every day because there's always something there too large to fit into my mailbox here. Not that I'm complaining. It's that time of year when you kind of expect to go a bit crazy.

It is not that time of year when I would expect to be spending my time contemplating my final moments and trying to make the "natural choice"—while still assuring that my family will be provided with the "utmost respect, sensitivity, and compassion they deserve."

Quite honestly, my arrangements were made years ago and revised slightly when I moved back to Georgia. My ex-wife has been relieved of her former responsibilities as "Grieving Widow", so she doesn't have to buy that long black dress after all. I will be cremated in Canton, Georgia—close your windows if you live in Canton. My ashes will then be divided in half. One half will be placed around some extremely healthy tree so that I can live on, vicariously, as part of an oak tree for example. The other half will be taken, with dignity (one would hope) up to my old hometown, Blue Earth, Minnesota, by my sons. There they will be given to my high school girlfriend, who will dump me one more time.

Don't you just love that joke? It came to me spontaneously when I was serving as Master of Ceremonies for our Fiftieth (?) High School Class Reunion. She asked, "When?" Was that nasty or what? But it sure got a laugh. I've since tried to talk her into joining me as part of a vaudeville team traveling the country to put on comedy shows, but her husband, Andy, doesn't care much for the idea. In fact, neither does she. I will never understand women. Never!

Anyhow, Neptune Society, remove 101 Corner Oak Court from your mailing list. It's all taken care of, and I have Christmas to worry about. After all, "Time stands still for no one."

12. And So The First Year Ends In This Log Cabin In The North Georgia Mountains

I tried to tell it honestly and well. There is, of course, much more that could be told, but time is a harsh task master, and as the poet Robert Frost once said, "I have miles to go before I sleep." I do hope that you have enjoyed traveling through this year with me, alone in this cabin.

Stories To The End Of Time

You might think it odd, perhaps, if you know me well, that I keep three Bibles in my old log cabin's library. It's not odd, at all. First, there is respect for ancestors who believed each word. Then, there is respect for my extended family, largely Christian by any measure, cousins and those they love. There is even greater respect for my own family—sons, grand-children, great-grandchildren—rising into a world so very different from my own. And there is respect for my many friends of all faiths, and great love for all who came before me and go on after me. The Bibles reflect that love and respect.

The Biblical book of Ecclesiastes, 31:8, tells us that to everything there is a season, and a time to every purpose under heaven. For me, it seems to be saying, "A time to write, and a time to refrain from writing." The year of aloneness I promised myself has been fulfilled, and these written stories are coming to an end even as the lives and times that led to them go on.

The book of stories was created because I was alone, for the very first time in my life, in this past year, divorced after forty years of marriage. It was my intent to share feelings, thoughts, joys, sorrows at age eighty-one while living alone for one full year in an old log cabin in the oak and pine forests of the North Georgia mountains. I planned to share only the first year of my aloneness, and so I have, and a wee bit more. The days and nights in this old log cabin have led to thoughts I never knew I'd have, to emotions, to love, and the loss of love, and tales of a large black cat, of a bear, of all those hungry deer. Those stories now belong to you.

It is now the season to end these stories. I'm still alone, except for a twelve pound, ten-year old cat, and family, helpers, and friends who are seeing me through a major illness, helping me move toward full health again, helping me to make it as a single guy learning about life in a different way than ever before. There has been great joy, deep thoughts, moments of sadness, and times of laughter. Through it all I have learned, like never before, the worth of caring friends and loving family. What a fine, fascinating year! The joy of their stories will go on to the end of time.

"To everything there is a season." Like you, I look forward to what the next season will bring.

—Beaumont R. "Ace" Hagebak
March, 2018

Feelin' Purly

No, this is not about cats. It's about health—more specifically, mine. Been feeling purrly for about three weeks now.

Once upon a time Georgia elected a true mountain man as Governor. He lived way up in the North Georgia mountains in a house built of rounded, water washed rocks that his mother dragged up from a nearby river. She actually built the house. Strong woman. We specialize in those up here in North Georgia. My wife was this Governor's Director of Aging Services state-wide and I was some kind of muckety-muck in the U.S. Public Health Service, so we got to know Governor Zell Miller fairly well. He often talked about doing more for the poor in our state, but he pronounced it "purr". Good enough for him, good enough for me,

Been feelin' a bit "purrly" lately. Kind of "off my feed", "not myself", "weak and heavy laden", "wiped out". The symptoms are interesting, at least to me. Exhaustion is the biggie. Get up, get cleaned up and dressed, and have to sit on the edge of the bed for a while. I make the bed because mom would have wanted me to, and then have to sit on the edge of the bed again. Take the hummingbird feeder out (It's inside at night to keep the deer from drinking it dry) and have to sit a bit. Make my coffee and the cat's breakfast—no problem, except that my hands are so palsied that I dribble more water onto the floor than into the cat's dish, Cold chills in the afternoon, with the thermostat set at 82 and me covered with a blanket. Can't do my normal chores around the cabin, can't even make dinner. Frozen dinners don't appeal, so it's chips and dip again tonight!

My Primary Care doc is moving away at the end of this week, but I think I've found a replacement. The new doc and I think this may be one of those "déjà vu" experiences: my thyroid coming back to haunt me. Many years ago, I developed these same symptoms while in Greece, got home, and just sat In my recliner all day, too exhausted to do much of anything. Once a day I drove to the grocery store, bought a lemon merangue pie (I have never learned to spell "marangue"), and ate the whole blessed thing myself! No interest in lemon yet this time around. And then, one afternoon, I went into a lead-walled room in a clinic somewhere, a nurse came in with two vials of liquid encased in lead, and I was told to drink the contents after she left the room. She also told me not to sleep in the same bed with my wife for three nights, "…or she'll begin to glow in the dark"! (A nursing joke, I think.) Radiation worked its wonders, dealt with the thyroid, and I was soon well enough to eat a pork chop again!

They drew four giant-sized vials of blood from me yesterday, to test our little thyroid theory and then some. They will call me back in a few days for a consult and maybe more blood. And that's what "feelin' purrly" will do to you. Not much fun. But my youngest son's wife is battling cancer, so this exhaustion of mine is "small potatoes" as they say. Keep her in your hearts.

Feelin' Purly, Part Two

Got a phone call Friday night, long after most outpatient facility people have gone home for the night. "The blood tests came back. You're anemic. Very low blood platelet count, low white blood cells count, and low red blood cells count. You seem to be functioning either on water or on red wine. Here's the name of a hematologist to call on Monday morning."

"Hematologist"? Why don't they just call them "blood doctors" and be done with it? I guess they need the prestige that only comes with a fancy title, but "endocrinologist" has them beat, and probably always will! Platelets? Those must be little tiny plates like the ones you have in your kitchen cupboard. Look closely. Platelets may have "Made In China" on the back. Ya' think?

And do we really need more cells, white or red? I think our judges are filling up the cells because they are trying to be tough on crime. Well, there are other ways of dealing with criminals. Frontal lobotomies come to mind. So what's this all about, anyhow?

Monday morning I will place a call to a hematologist with a name that sounds like it was invented by a writer for *Star Wars* , and who probably will feel the same way about "Hagebak". Whenever I get called by a nurse to leave my comfortable chair and magazine in the waiting room to walk back to heaven knows what awaits me on the other side of that door, they always say "Beaumont"? I get up, walk toward them in a menacing manner, and ask, "Why so familiar?? I've never met you before. Didn't dare to say my last name, did you?" Usually they will break down and confess that they were afraid to try it. Then I grin and help them out a bit. It's "Hag—uh—back". They always seem grateful.

So…it's not the thyroid at all. It's actually more difficult to treat. Blood platelets, for example, are apparently made by bone marrow. Doctors need a small drill to get through bone to the marrow. The whole thought makes me weak.

Oh, yah. That's how all this started in the first place. I am weak as a kitten, and not nearly as cute. Keep me in your thoughts. Maybe you can help me escape to Canada? I hear that there's a wall being built in the other direction. Thanks.

Epilogue

The Bear went over the Mountain

Here at the cabin in the woods, there's a sign out front warning all visitors "Den Gammel Bjorn Lair", the old bear's den. The cabin has been a perfect place for the old bear to hibernate, eat, and rest... as bears are known to do. There's also a cat to keep the bear entertained. Other woodland animals would stop by often to see the Gammel Bjorn. At first, they entered the den with some caution, no other occupant of the den had been so social. This "new" old bear shared his odd bear food and expanded the palate, tastes and familiarity with all things bear related. The tales of the bear spread quickly and visitors come from far and wide to spend time with the bear, to watch the bear scratch his back on the pine bark, engage in bizarre eating habits that universally included cheese and red wine, and be entertained by the habitat the bear created that attracted deer, birds, chipmunks, rabbits, and some much-hated squirrels. The bear seemed to care for the woods, in turn, the woods provided for the bear. A really symbiotic relationship.

You probably know the words to the old song, "*The Bear went over the Mountain*" which has been inexorably linked to the tune of "*For He's A Jolly Good Fellow*". In the tune, the bear crosses the mountain, a river and a meadow and all that he could see was the other side. The bear meets another bear in this faraway place. The song ends with the bears playing and unfortunately, the bear does not return.

The bear that once lived at Corner Oak Court has left his den and won't be returning. He's gone over the mountain, the river, the meadow. The woodland animals will miss being fed so well. The squirrels near the den have stolen most of the bird seed in preparation for the winter that is just weeks away. The frequent visitors of the bear's den will miss the bear. These visitors were so much more than guests, these were the bear's extended family. The bear really loved everyone who visited or sent notes to his den, he really did. Perhaps no one will miss the Gammel Bjorn more than his three cubs; never ready to say goodbye to the old bear, unsure they will be ready for the forest without him. But the Gammel Bjorn prepared his cubs well and they will continue to imitate the old bear by being accepting and inviting to other woodland animals.

The Gammel Bjorn has gone over the mountain and the tough truth is that he'll never return to his old den.

Dr. Beaumont Roger "Ace" Hagebak passed away in the early evening of the 1st of November 2018, working on correspondence on his computer, enjoying a glass of wine. A memorial gathering of friends, family, and other woodland creatures is being arranged. As soon as we have a date, time and location of this gathering, Ace's "cubs" will share that information with you.

Thank you for being a friend to our family.

Beaumont, Christen, and Haakon

Following Is The Obituary Ace Wrote For The Atlanta Journal-Constitution...

HAGEBAK, Dr. Beaumont Roger—Dr. Beaumont R. Hagebak of Waleska, died of natural causes on Friday, November 2, 2018. He was 82 years of age. He wrote this obituary, so members of his family are blameless. (About this, at least.) Born in Starbuck, Minnesota to Norwegian-American parents, he was a product of small-town America. He spent most of his formative years in Blue Earth, Minnesota, where he graduated from high school in 1954. He still considers Blue Earth to be his hometown. After two years with the U.S. Army, serving in the post-World War II Occupation Forces in Garmisch, Germany where he learned to stand at attention while not totally sober, he returned home to enroll at the University of Northern Iowa, Cedar Falls, Iowa. There he earned his Bachelor's degree in education, and Master's degree in school counseling. While still in college he met and married Lillian Kate Price of Grinnell, Iowa. The couple had three sons before dissolving their marriage in 1976. Dr. Hagebak began his career as a high school guidance counselor in Reinbeck, Iowa in 1961. After two years of learning how very little he really knew about helping teenagers, he enrolled in the doctoral counseling psychology program at Arizona State University, Tempe and earned his doctorate there in 1967. In 1964, while working on his doctoral dissertation, he relocated his family to his home state of Minnesota, where he became an Associate Professor of Psychology and Director of the Psychological Services Center at Mankato State University. The Center prospered under his leadership, and that success led to his appointment as Dean of Students at Northland College in Ashland, Wisconsin in 1969. Those were difficult times in the academic world, and Dr. Hagebak was formally introduced to the student body by the then-President of the Student Government as a "racist, fascist pig". Three years later, before leaving the frozen north for Georgia, Dr.

Hagebak served as best man in the wedding of the next President of that same Student Government. He saw that as progress. In 1971, when he finally realized that Georgia was warmer than northern Wisconsin, Dr. Hagebak moved his family to LaGrange to become the first community mental health center director in a thirteen county health district just south of Atlanta. After he drew in a couple of million Federal dollars for that cause, he was promoted to manage all public health, mental health, welfare and vocational rehabilitation services in the same area. That proved to be such a pleasant chore that he was promoted again, and took on 54 counties in western Georgia, directing all of their Department of Human Resources services. A 'chief' rather than an "Indian", Dr. Hagebak's job was eliminated in a purge of administrators ordered by then-Governor George Busbee. Then his father died, the divorce happened, and he started dating again. (Funny business, that.) Eventually, he met and married Judith Eve (Mertz) Hula, of Marietta, Georgia, and merged the two families. Judy had a son by a previous marriage. It was a great marriage but ended in a mutually agreed-upon divorce in 2017. Dr. Hagebak then served as an Atlanta-based human services consultant for a year or so, before joining the U.S. Public Health Service, Atlanta Regional Office, as a Mental Health Program Consultant for NIMH in eight southern states. Eventually Ronald Reagan, then-President of the United States, shut down all of the Regional Offices of NIMH in the mistaken belief that mental diseases had been cured nationwide. Dr. Hagebak was permitted to stay on when all of his colleagues were fired, because he was a military veteran. Guilt-ridden, he wrote a couple of books during this period, since there was little else to do. Eventually, though, he moved up in the system and became the Deputy Regional Health Administrator for Region IV—Alabama, Florida, Georgia, Kentucky, Mississippi, North Carolina, South Carolina, and Tennessee. His most shining hour was when Hurricane Andrew hit Miami, and he was in charge of the federal public health response. It was quite exciting to watch the parade of Republican big shots marching through the disaster area. Not a pretty sight. Sort of like cleaning up after the circus goes through your hometown. "Grab the shovels, men, here comes another one!" Some of the finest people he ever knew were U.S. Public Health Services personnel! He retired from the Federal government in 1999, moved to a log cabin in the North Georgia mountains, and did a little consulting on emergency preparedness until the Bush administration set up the Department of Homeland Security and made a royal mess of things. Then he took up watercolor painting and began teaching psychology at North Georgia College and State University in Dahlonega. Some years later he and his wife moved to Roswell, Georgia, and he began to teach human growth and development in the Psychology Department at Kennesaw State University. He used his own personnel experiences in his teaching since he had lived, at the time, all of the stages of human growth except death and dying. He and his wife traveled a bit, too, visiting Norway, Sweden, Denmark, France, Germany, Austria, Italy, Greece, Japan, China, England, and Scotland using the money he earned from teaching. He didn't really earn much from watercoloring, but it kept him out of the bars and off the streets in his old age. So did his efforts to document the genealogy of his Hagebak and Mork families, which led to three books about them, and a smaller book about his mother, "Go-Go Gertie" (Gertrude Hagebak). In 2011 Dr. Hagebak (then age 75) and his wife moved to Roseville, California to watch their two-year-old granddaughter grow up and to see and do new and interesting things in a totally different part of the country. it was hard leaving family and friends behind in Georgia, but exciting to deal with such a major change so late in life. He loved living in California, and with his wife toured the western coastal area, created a backyard nature preserve, served on the steering committee of the community wine tasting club, and met wonderful new friends (most, but not all, Democrats). Together, he and Judy traveled to Europe several times. They particularly loved river cruises. In 2016, as they were nearing their 40th wedding anniversary, he and Judy decided, for a variety of reasons to divorce. Their divorce was final in 2017, and he moved back East to be closer to his own family. It was a tough time for both of them. Eventually, at age 80, he settled in an old log cabin in the Lake Arrowhead Community near Waleska, Georgia, in the foothills of the North Georgia mountains. Dr. Hagebak was a proud member of the American Humanist Society, Americans United for Separation of Church and State, the Wilderness Society and several other environmental organizations, the Democratic National Committee, and other progressive groups. He thoroughly enjoyed being well left of center, religiously and politically, and loved to yell at Republicans and evangelical Christians appearing on television. He also yelled at people who drove too slowly in the left lane. Often they were the same people. Dr. Hagebak, or "Ace" as he was called throughout his lifetime because of an unfortunate incident in eighth grade involving a huge paper airplane in study hall, is survived by his sons Beaumont William, Christen Daane, Haakon Price; their delightful spouses, five beautiful and bright granddaughters, and a fine set of great-grandchildren. He was preceded in death by his parents, Dr. C. Beaumont H. Hagebak and Gertrude E. (Mork) Hagebak, and by his kid sister, Corinne A. (Hagebak) Grussing. A memorial program (certainly not a religious service) is being planned for Friday, November 16th at 11:30a.m., at the Lake Arrowhead Club House, complete with hors d'oeuvres, a bit of wine, and absolutely no piano music. He had to suffer through piano lessons in the third grade, and hated them and the piano ever since! Memorial contributions may be made to any activist environmental organization that seeks to preserve endangered wildlife, the shrinking wilderness areas in the United States, or to expand urban green space at the expense of urban and suburban developers. As an alternative, people can also donate memorial funds to Vesterheim, the Norwegian-American folk museum in Decorah, Iowa; or to the Lac qui

Parle County Historical Museum in Madison, Minnesota where artifacts that once belonged to members of Dr. Hagebak's pioneer family are
displayed. (Look up the addresses on the internet, OK?) Darby Funeral
Home.

Published in The Atlanta Journal-Constitution on Nov. 9, 2018

Our father left very specific and copious instructions for me and my brothers
relating to his memorial program, cremation, finances, and the like. Not a
single item was missed, right down to the order of music and readings. It was
a blessing and a curse—my brothers and I had so many things to do to satisfy
dad's wishes, but it seemed a small price to pay to honor such an interesting
father. These notes were penned by dad on December 5, 2016 and were sealed
and unseen by anyone until they were read aloud by his good friend Bruce
Whyte at his memorial program on November 16, 2018 at the Lake Arrow-
head Clubhouse.

Notes To Be Read Aloud By A Friend At The Memorial Program For Beaumont R. Hagebak

Well, it's good of you to all come to this memorial program. Wish I
was with you. Who knows? Perhaps I am. In any case, I have asked that
there be some fairly heavy hors d'oevres and a bit of wine and beer for
you when it's over. I would have enjoyed that myself, as you know, so fill
your plate and your glass, tell a story or two, make a play on words now
and then as I would have done, and enjoy the rest of the day. Wherever I
am I may be doing that too. If there is an afterlife it simply must include
heavy hors d'oevres, a bit of wine, and a play on words or two. If not, I'll
really be out of my element!

Speaking of the afterlife leads me to consider with you my humanist
values. Sometimes I envy those family members and friends who seem

to know with utter certainty that a God exists who will afford them everlasting life. Such faith must offer a real sense of peace. Me? I am just a humanist with a bunch of questions. Since my late 20s, I have been unable to do the "blind faith" thing. If a person, like me, can't accept the traditional Christian belief system, then it's impossible to have faith in such a system. So, beyond the age of 30 or so, I never had that sort of faith. It was late in my life that I discovered humanism, and found that it was something I could believe.

The American Humanist Association defines it this way: "Humanism is a rational philosophy informed by science, inspired by art, and motivated by compassion. Affirming the dignity of each human being, it supports liberty and opportunity consistent with social and planetary responsibility. Free of theism and other supernatural beliefs, humanism thus derives the goals of life from human need and interest rather than from theological or ideological abstractions, and asserts that humanity must take responsibility for its own destiny."

That means, of course, that I doubt that there will be any sort of afterlife for me or for anyone. However I must say that if I'm wrong and a loving all-knowing God does exist, though (the only kind I would have any dealings with in any case), that sort of God would understand my difficulty with doctrinal faith and exclusionary creeds, and my aspiration's for human beings, and will lovingly make room for me in Wherever. It is with that faith that I died. Religions of the world are so diverse and numerous. God must appreciate diversity. If so, then my simple faith in human beings should be sufficiently diverse to guarantee me a spot in Wherever!

Kurt Vonnegut was a humorist, author, and rather irreverent humanist. He was once the honorary president of the American Humanist Association. I've always enjoyed his work. In his 1997 book, *Timequake*, written when he was 78 years old, Vonnegut described my own view quite well. He said, on page 72 , "Humanists try to behave decently and honorably without any expectation of rewards or punishments in the afterlife. The creator of the universe has been unknowable to us thus far. We serve as well as we can the highest abstraction of which we have some understanding, which is our community." Vonnegut went on to say, "I like to sleep. It is no bad thing to want to sleep for everyone as in afterlife. I see no need up in the Sky for more torture chambers and bingo games."

I always sort of enjoyed that notion. Life everlasting as a giant bingo game in the Sky! Under the "B", Beaumont Roger Hagebak! Not likely. But I suppose there is that "if". So if I am a winner, and get to heaven of some sort, and if you are there too, I'll make you the same promise that I made to my mother just before she died. I promise to tiptoe past your mansion, so as not to embarrass you! Mom laughed. I hope you did just now, too.

But on the other hand, perhaps my Viking forbearers have prepared a place at the table for me in their Valhalla! Mead, smoked pork ribs, some lefsa, a wandering minstrel or two, several gorgeous blonde Valkyries...now that wouldn't be bad at all! Maybe you could visualize me now, seated at the big wooden table in Valhalla, checking the door every once in a while in the hope that you'll walk through to join me there...Because I am really going to miss you, wherever I am or not now.

I've made just a few requests for those who planned this memorial program (it is not a "memorial service"). Knowing me, you'll realize that "just a few requests" from me is pretty unusual. And while I did suggest some special readings and music, I normally would have planned this event right down to the complete agenda...Correct? But one has to give up on obsessive compulsive behaviors at some point, and for me, death seemed to be the most appropriate time!

I did request that this last speech of mine be read aloud by someone who enjoys public speaking almost as much as I did, and who knew me well enough to enjoy sharing my final words with those assembled here.

Goodness knows, I'd rather be reading the speech myself! But thanks, my friend, anyway.

I also ask that no piano music be played during this thing. There are those of you who love piano music and you're welcome to your opinions. Me? Ever since I was forced to take piano lessons as a child, one of my goals in life has been to purchase a piano and chop it into bits with a sledgehammer! That goal has remained unfulfilled because, when I finally became wealthy enough to purchase a piano, I was just too tight with my money to allow myself that luxury. Somewhere out there, there's a piano that should consider itself damned lucky! And, if…by some error…a piano has intruded on the sanctity of this memorial service, then I refuse to be held responsible for anything that might happen!

I've also asked that someone willing to accept and understand my humanistic views serve as the leader of this memorial program. So many religions and denominations seem arrogant to me, when they profess that their way is the only way! Arrogance, in my view, is the greatest sin of all…Particularly when dealing with the unknowable.

I do believe strongly in the Unitarian Universalist concept of the "independent web of all existence", and have tried to attest to the dignity and worth of every individual. That said, I personally do not believe that the "dignity and worth of every individual" notion applies to people who drive too slowly in the left hand lane. It's particularly alright to yell at such persons, and I did at every opportunity! Yelling at those people, and the conservative Republicans of course, was one of the great joys of my life! (Often they were the same folks, anyhow.)

Well, I would like you to know that I have learned a few important things in this life that I have lived. I learned that I love to teach. I learned that it is important to shower every day. I learned to cook some pretty decent pork ribs. But the most important thing I ever learned was to finally understand just how vital the love of family and friends is to living the good life. I came to that great truth only in midlife, I'm sorry to say until I was in my late 40s, I was so focused on my own self-centered needs for status and power that I failed to fully appreciate what life was truly about. Glad that I finally figured that out! You, my friends and family, you gave my life its real meaning. You made my life so wonderful.

There have been people who I've grown close to, and who have a special place in my mind and heart. I've done the friendship of some wonderful men, the love of some beautiful ladies, and the affection of some great children and grandchildren!

My sons and their delightful wives have been very important people in my life, also. We are close, but not cloyingly close. We come together in times of celebration and in times of trouble, but we allow one another the space to move independently through our separate lives at the same time. I always wanted my sons to be secure and happy. For the most part, that has been the case. We would worry from time to time, of course, because that is what parents do. But worry doesn't help much. As Haakon once said when he was a youngster and didn't get home at the time he was expected for supper, "Well, you shouldn't have been worried about me. I knew where I was!" Each of you, my sons, always know where you are in the world, always experience love, and always be in a joyous place! Each of you, in his own delightfully unique way, has made me a proud and happy man! I will always love you, my sons.

And my wonderful granddaughters, I loved you all. You know that. Saga and Annabelle Grace have one special aspect that gives me great joy—they each carry a genetic bit of me that will go into the unknown future. I want you to know that I get a kick out of being part of who you are, and that I walk with you up life's winding genetic trail. But all of my granddaughters were deeply loved, Shannon, Savannah, and Stacie, you too were super "cool" as my very own granddaughters. And now my great grandchildren—they are great! I wish all good things for you.

You—all of your grandchildren and great grandchildren—may view my life and times as "antiquated" or, at the very least, "quaint". But you will always be my family! Family has been a special interest of mine because it has been findable, and because it tells us something of who we are. Our family tree, stretching back to ancient Norway, links us all on a march back through time to a place before births and deaths were even recorded. And that's just the past! The future calls you grandchildren—it's less knowable to an old guy like your "Pappa Ace", but I'll bet that it will be exciting, and that you'll each do well with the challenges you find in it. I will always love you all my grandchildren and great grandchildren. All of you.

Well, if all has gone according to plan, my poor old body has been cremated in my half. One half of my remains will one day be placed around a giant suitable long lived tree, so I can nourish the tree and become part of its long life. Half of my remains will be buried in a Cemetery in Blue Earth, Minnesota, a little farming community in southern Minnesota that I've always felt was "home". I hope, my family and friends, that when you visit someplace you love most in the world you might think of me and think that we're both in a place very special to us to be occasionally in your thoughts...That's immortality.

SKOAL!!

Photographs

Bear visits the Old Bear's Den

Deer at the Old Bear's Den

(left to right) The author, Stacie Schnurrer, Nelaina Schnurrer
(grand daughter and great grand daughter)

(left to right) The author's sons, Haakon, Beaumont, Christen

The author, center, US Army, Venice Italy

The author in Ball Ground, GA

The author, cruise of Norway, 2015

Acknowledgements

Bruce M. Whyte, M.d. put this manuscript into an electronic form, re-quested by reviewers reading the document for publication. Bruce is a friend of long-standing. He and his wife, Kathy, live in Roswell, Georgia.

Mark Taylor volunteered to make use of his skills as a former English teacher to review the manuscript, making corrections in spelling, punc-tuation, and grammar. Mark and his wife, Betsy, are new friends and live down the road a piece from the author.

Friends And Relatives, about fifty of them, were on an e-mail list to receive drafts of each story as it was written. Their comments and sug-gestions on content were all valuable, and their positive perspectives on the writings gave encouragement to the author that was sorely needed at times.

About the Author

Born and raised in Minnesota, Dr. Beaumont R. Hagebak joined the U.S. Army in 1954 and served in the Occupation of Germany. He earned his Bachelor's and Master's degrees at the University of Northern Iowa, and his Doctorate in Counseling Psychology at Arizona State University. He became Director of the Psychological Services Center at Mankato State University (MN), then Dean at Northland College (WI). In 1972, he relocated to Georgia to work with Governor Carter's administration, developing community mental health facilities throughout the state. He joined the U.S. Public Health Service in 1977 and rose to Acting Regional Health Administrator for an eight state region of the South. Upon retirement, he served as an Adjunct Professor of Psychology in Georgia's university system for ten years. He then retired to California, where his wife of 40 years asked for a divorce, and at age 80, he moved back to Georgia to be near his three sons and their families. He lives in a log cabin in the North Georgia mountains with a large black cat. He is the author of several professional and family history books and many journal articles. He now writes and does watercolor portraits as he tries to age gracefully.